Glimpses
of God

Glimpses of God

Revealed through His Names

DEBI PRYDE

REGULAR BAPTIST PRESS
1300 North Meacham Road
Schaumburg, Illinois 60173-4806

Dedication

*To all my Sunday School teachers who instilled a love
for the Word of God when I was a child,
and to my husband, the best Bible teacher I have ever known.*

ACKNOWLEDGMENTS:

"His Name Is Wonderful" ©1959 Audrey Mieir. Renewed 1987 Manna Music, Inc. (35255 Brooten Road, Pacific City, OR 97135).

"He's Able" ©1958 New Spring Publishing (Brentwood-Benson Music Publishing, Inc. Admin. by Music Services, Inc., 5409 Maryland Way, Ste 200, Brentwood, TN 37027). Used by permission. All rights reserved.

"Surely Goodness and Mercy" ©1954 New Spring Publishing (Brentwood-Benson Music Publishing, Inc. Admin. by Music Services, Inc., 5409 Maryland Way, Ste 200, Brentwood, TN 37027). Used by permission. All rights reserved.

"Seek Ye First" ©1972 Maranatha! Music (Admin. by Music Services, Inc., 5409 Maryland Way, Ste 200, Brentwood, TN 37027). Used by permission. All rights reserved.

"I Sing a New Song" ©1974 New Spring Publishing (Brentwood-Benson Music Publishing, Inc. Admin. by Music Services, Inc., 5409 Maryland Way, Ste 200, Brentwood, TN 37027). Used by permission. All rights reserved.

Contents

Preface

If love, joy, peace, longsuffering, gentleness, goodness, faith, humility, and self-control could be purchased, would you stand in line to pay whatever it cost to buy them? What price would you pay to fill your life with grace and peace and all the wonderful characteristics of God's divine nature?

What if I were to tell you that grace and peace and everything that pertains to living a successful Christian life could be yours abundantly simply by knowing God? Would you be interested?

Good news! The Word of God tells us, "Grace and peace be multiplied unto you through the knowledge of God, and of Jesus our Lord, According as his divine power hath given unto us all things that pertain unto life and godliness, through the knowledge of him that hath called us to glory and virtue: Whereby are given unto us exceeding great and precious promises: that by these ye might be partakers of the divine nature, having escaped the corruption that is in the world through lust" (2 Peter 1:2–4).

When speaking of the innumerable benefits and mysteries of knowing God, the apostle Paul exclaimed, "O the depth of the riches both of the wisdom and knowledge of God!" (Romans 11:33). God is so wonderful, vast, great, and complex that we could never exhaust all there is to know about Him. Neither could we measure in silver or gold the worth of knowing and understanding Him. That God reveals Himself so freely and makes knowledge of His ways so readily available to mankind is in itself an incredible gift. And, as if that is not astounding enough, God offers something even more marvelous—a loving, intimate relationship with Him.

We begin our study of eleven Old Testament names of God by first pondering the Biblical significance of names. As we progress, we will learn how knowing God's names strengthens our love, faith, and confidence in God and results in delight and joy in Him. "O magnify the LORD with me, and let us exalt his name together" (Psalm 34:3).

How to Use This Study

Each lesson in this study is divided into four parts. Follow these suggestions as you prepare each lesson.

Key Verse

The key verse or verses are the ones at the beginning of the lesson. Memorize the verse(s) and think about them during the day. Review the verses from previous lessons to keep them fresh in your mind and to think about how the verses interrelate.

Study the Word

Read the introductions, answer the questions, and read the commentary. Think about how the facts apply to your life.

Concluding Thoughts

This part is a summary of the lesson truths. Again, think about how these truths apply to your life right now. What will you do to employ them?

Express the Truth in Song

This section offers a verse and a hymn or song. Think about the words of each. If you know the hymn or song, sing it to God as worship and thanksgiving. If you are musical, consider putting the verse from Psalms to music to sing yourself or to teach to the other women in your Bible study.

What's in a Name?

"Therefore my people shall know my name: therefore they shall know in that day that I am he that doth speak: behold, it is I" (Isaiah 52:6).

The Christian life is not a religion. It is a deeply personal relationship with the Creator of the universe and the Savior of all mankind. It is a relationship like no other, for it satisfies our human longing to be known, understood, and loved. Best of all, it is a relationship in which we are invited to intimately know, understand, and love our God. God wants us to know Him! He is immensely pleased when we take an interest in knowing and understanding Him! So it is that He introduced Himself to us and began to paint a lovely portrait of Himself by telling us His names and showing us in rich detail their significance.

William Shakespeare wrote in *Romeo and Juliet*, "A rose by any other name would smell as sweet."[1] By this he meant that the flower's name is not significant when it comes to the flower's fragrance. Likewise for Juliet, Romeo's name was unimportant.

However, as children, we women may have discovered differently. When someone called us "fatso" or "stupid," no matter how often we invoked the "sticks and stones may break my bones, but names will never hurt me" mantra, the names still stung. For us the names mattered.

The corporate world understands the importance of a name. Corporations spend billions of dollars each year solely to ensure that consumers understand the significance of a company's brand on a product. Corporate balance sheets list and value all their assets, including their brands. "Brand equity" describes the premium (or discount) that a product can command, as compared to its competitors, by virtue of its brand name. For corporations (and consumers!) brand names mean something about the value or performance that can be expected from products.

STUDY THE WORD

Names in the Bible

In the Bible, names often have special significance.

1. Explain the name that Adam gave his wife (Genesis 3:20).

EVE, because she was the mother of all living.

Adam named his third son Seth (meaning "compensation") because Eve believed God had given her another son to take the place of Abel, who had been killed by Cain (Genesis 4:25). Later, Lamech named his son Noah (meaning "rest") because he believed Noah would bring comfort (rest) from curse-induced toil (5:29). Sometimes people received new names because of significant changes in their circumstances (e.g., Abram/Abraham, Genesis 17:5; Sarai/Sarah, Genesis 17:15; Jacob/Israel, Genesis 32:28).

Even place names often had special significance. The city of Zoar (meaning "insignificance") is an example. Lot wanted to take refuge in that small, unimportant city before God destroyed Sodom and Gomorrah (Genesis 19:22). Zoar's significance was its insignificance!

2. Another place-name involved Isaac. He separated from the herdsmen of Gerar to avoid a conflict over some wells (Genesis 26:19–22).
   (a) What did he call the third place (v. 22)?

   Rehoboth -'...

   (b) Why did he give it that name? *for the Lord made room for us and we shall be fruitful in the land.*

3. Read Genesis 28:12–22 and 35:11–15. Why did Jacob call the place where he slept Bethel, or house of God? What significant events took place there? *God spoke to him, choosing him & his seed to multiply; for a nation shall come from Jacob.*

4. Sometimes people changed their own names. Read Ruth 1:19–21.
The name "Naomi" means "pleasant" or "delight."
(a) Why d–id Naomi change her name to Mara?
— the Lord brought her home empty. Mara - means bitter

(b) Why do you suppose God continued to call her Naomi? —
because God knew her future.

Of course, Old Testament men and women did not look through the *Baby Book of Names* to choose interesting names for their children. Biblical names were deliberately chosen for specific reasons. Four common ones were (1) to describe the child at his or her birth, the circumstances, or impressions surrounding the child's birth; (2) to state the child's purpose or future mission; (3) to illustrate a special message of God; to express that person's connection with God or faith in God; (4) to express someone's authority over another or a change in someone's situation or destiny.

These four reasons are illustrated in questions 5–10.

5. How do each of the following names describe the child at birth, the circumstances, or impressions surrounding the birth?
Peleg (Genesis 10:25) – *for in his days the earth was divided.*

Isaac (Genesis 17:17; 18:12) *they were old beyond child bearing age.*

Esau (Genesis 25:24, 25) — *born first and had hair all over like a hairy garment.*

Jacob (Genesis 25:26; 27:36) – *took hold of Esau's heel, took away Esau's birth rights & blessing.*

6. "Solomon" means "peace." Read 1 Chronicles 22:8 and 9. How did

Solomon's name reflect the characteristics of his future reign?

7. "Jesus" means "Savior." What did Jesus' name reveal about His purpose on earth (Matthew 1:21)?

8. God told Hosea what to name his three children to illustrate a special message from God. According to the book of Hosea, why were they given these names?
   1:4—Jezreel ("God sows")

   1:6—Loruhamah ("no mercy")

   1:9—Loammi ("not my people")

9. Read Genesis 17:5. How did the change in Abram's name (which means "father") express Abraham's authority over another or a change in his situation or destiny?

10. Read Daniel 1:5–7.
    (a) Who changed the names of the four Hebrew men, and what did he change them to?

        "Daniel" was changed to _Belteshazzar_

        "Hananiah" was changed to _Shadrach_.

        "Mishael" was changed to _Meshach_.

"Azariah" was changed to _____Abednego._____ .

(b) Read Genesis 41:45. Who changed Joseph's name, and what did he change it to?

Names of God in the Old Testament

Throughout mankind's existence, God has chosen different ways to reveal Himself to us: through His creation (Psalm 19:1–6; Romans 1:20, 21), through His prophets and by the words and works of His Son Jesus Christ (Hebrews 1:1, 2), and through His written Word (2 Timothy 3:16; 2 Peter 1:19–21). One of the ways God reveals Himself in the Scriptures is through His names.

- The name "Elohim" speaks of God's power and tells us that God is able to meet our needs in any situation.
- "El Elyon" tells of His majesty and sovereignty over all things, reminding us that God is the triumphant ruler over all the earth.
- "El Roi" tells of God's ability to see everything, including each of us, wherever we are.
- "El Shaddai" refers to an Almighty God who is sufficient in every way.
- "Jehovah" reminds us that God is a personal God who is all powerful and works on our behalf.
- "Jehovah-Rohi" is the Shepherd of our souls, who guides and meticulously cares for His own throughout life's journey.
- "Jehovah-Sabaoth" reminds us that God goes into battle with His children and secures their victory.
- The name "Jehovah-Tsidkenu" describes the God who is perfectly righteous and who clothes believers in His righteousness, giving them unconditional acceptance in His presence.
- "Adonai" is the name that reminds us that God is our Master to Whom we willingly submit.

These are nine of the most well-known names of God found in the Old Testament. We will study these names in more depth in future lessons.

Three Important Names

The Old Testament uses three primary Hebrew names for God that will be important to remember throughout our study. These three names are Elohim, Yahweh (also transliterated Jehovah), and Adonai. Each name speaks of a different attribute of God and His relationship to His people. In many English translations of the Bible, these three names are differentiated using different capitalization. The name "Jehovah" is translated both as "GOD" and "LORD," depending on the context, but it is always represented with a capital letter and small capital letters. The name "Elohim" is usually written "God," and Adonai is generally written "Lord" or "Sovereign." Thus you know that "LORD God" is a translation of "Yahweh Elohim," that "Lord GOD" is a translation of "Adonai Jehovah," and that "Lord God" is a translation of "Adonai Elohim."

Note how the Hebrew name "Adonai" appears in this English translation of the Bible as "Lord"; Jehovah in all caps as "GOD"; and the name "Elohim" as "God." Deuteronomy 10:17 illustrates these uses. "For the LORD [Jehovah] your God [Elohim] is God [Elohim] of gods, and Lord [Adonai] of lords."

11. Read the following verses and identify which name of God appears in each: Adonai, Jehovah, or Elohim.

    Psalm 147:5

    Genesis 1:1

    Exodus 6:6

12. Names ending in "iah" or "jah" refer to Jehovah, and names ending in "el" refer to God. For example, "Elijah" means "Jehovah is God," and "Jeremiah" means "Jehovah has appointed." How do the names "Israel" and "Samuel" express the owner's connection with God or faith in God?
    Genesis 32:28; 35:10—Israel ("a prince of God")

1 Samuel 1:20—Samuel ("asked of God")

13. Read Isaiah 7:14 and Matthew 1:23. What does the name "Immanuel" ("Emmanuel" in the New Testament) reveal to us about *who* Christ is?

14. In light of what you have learned about the significance of names in the Bible and according to John 3:18 and 20:31, what does it mean to believe in the name of the Son of God (Jesus)?

15. Read Acts 4:10–12 and Romans 10:13.
    (a) Is it possible to call upon any name other than Jesus Christ to receive salvation?

    (b) Why or why not?

Knowing and understanding God's names helps us to learn who God is and to respond in appropriate awe and adoration. The more we understand the significance of His names, the more we will understand how He meets the needs of our hearts.

16. Read Psalm 9:10. Describe how knowing God better enables you to trust Him in your daily life.

CONCLUDING THOUGHTS

Names in the Bible are meaningful, giving us a greater appreciation and understanding of Scripture. Yet no collection of names has more meaning or imparts more understanding than the many names of God.

Knowing and understanding His names helps us know and understand Him, for our God cannot be described by comparing Him to any one thing, let alone by characterizing Him by one name or attribute. Nothing in our world that we could compare Him to describes Him exactly. He asks, "To whom will ye liken me, and make me equal, and compare me, that we may be like?" (Isaiah 46:5). Our God is unique and so great that no human description can ever adequately convey His beauty and wonder. Yet He delights to give us a little glimpse into His heart by revealing Himself through the names He has given to Himself in His Word.

EXPRESS THE TRUTH IN SONG

"I will praise the name of God with a song, and will magnify him with thanksgiving" (Psalm 69:30).

His Name Is Wonderful

His name is Wonderful, His name is Wonderful,
His name is Wonderful, Jesus my Lord;
He is the mighty King, master of everything,
His name is Wonderful, Jesus, my Lord.

He's the great Shepherd, the Rock of all ages,
Almighty God is He;
Bow down before Him, love and adore Him,
His name is Wonderful, Jesus, my Lord.

—Audrey Mieir

Note:

1. William Shakespeare, *Romeo and Juliet,* 2.2.1–2.

"I AM"

*"And God said unto Moses, I AM THAT I AM: and he said,
Thus shalt thou say unto the children of Israel, I AM hath
sent me unto you" (Exodus 3:14).*

What thoughts come to mind when you hear the name "Plato,"
"Hitler," or "Abraham Lincoln"? These names evoke a response
because they represent not only certain people, but also the ideals for which they stood. The name we are going to consider in this lesson
is one that has enormous meaning, though at first glance it seems quite
unusual, if not puzzling. It is actually a summary of all that God is, and it
sets the stage for an unfolding revelation about Him. Our understanding
of this particular name helps us appreciate the importance of *all* of God's
names, so it is a good place to begin our study.

STUDY THE WORD

1. Look up the word "memorial" in a dictionary; then read Exodus
   3:14 and 15.
   (a) What does the word "memorial" mean (v. 15)?

   (b) What did God mean when He said that His name "I AM" is a
   memorial to all generations?

What Is His Name?

After four hundred years of Egyptian bondage, the Children of Israel
were about to be delivered out of slavery. God prepared Moses to lead them
out of Egypt into a land He had promised to them many years before. As

17

Moses contemplated meeting with God's people to tell them of His intention to free them, he asked God what he should tell them when they asked His name (Exodus 3:13). Moses' question seems a bit strange, but God's reply seems even stranger. He told Moses, "I AM THAT I AM" (v. 14). Then He said to tell the people "I AM" sent you. We'll explore what Moses meant by his question and what God was communicating in His reply. But first, let's look closely at the statement "I AM THAT I AM." It must have grabbed Moses' attention. God had never identified Himself by these words before. Furthermore, it is nothing a created being such as man could ever say about himself. God was saying, "I am the self-existing one." Unlike everything in our world, including ourselves, God had no origin, no cause, and no source from which He appeared. Our human minds struggle to comprehend: God came from nowhere; He is and always has been exactly what He is!

2. Read John 5:26 and Acts 17:25. Where does all life come from?

3. Read John 1:1–5 and Colossians 1:16 and 17.
   (a) Did Christ begin His life in Bethlehem?

   (b) Why or why not?

4. Read John 8:56–58.
   (a) What was Christ teaching about Himself?

   (b) How does this make Christ different from the religious figures who founded many of the world's religions?

When God stated, "I AM THAT I AM," He was saying not only that He is self-existent, but that He is unlike anything we can compare Him to. There is no way to adequately define God. He has many attributes, but an attribute is not a "part" of God—it is something God *is*. God is not loving one minute, just and righteous the next, and merciful another moment. He is the essence of all these and other wonderful attributes all at the same time, all of the time. He doesn't become more of *anything,* for God is eternal, perfect, and therefore complete. He is what He is and always has been.

5. Read Malachi 3:6. What important attribute did God reveal about Himself in this verse?

6. Read 1 John 4:8 and 16. How do these statements differ: "God is loving," and "God is love"?

7. Read Psalms 99:9 and 116:5. List four attributes of God found in these passages.

8. Read the following verses of Scripture. What does God tell us about Himself in each verse?
Genesis 15:1

Genesis 15:7

Genesis 17:1

Exodus 6:7

Exodus 22:27

Isaiah 43:3

Jeremiah 3:12

Who Says So?

When Moses asked God what he should tell the Israelites when they asked, "What is his name?" he was not merely inquiring what name God called Himself. From a Hebrew perspective, the question asks about the character and nature of the name. Moses was concerned that the Children of Israel would want to know *by what authority* he spoke and *the relationship of that authority* to the people. Theologian Edward J. Young restated Moses' question this way: "Was the God who made promises to the patriarchs still with His people and was he able to deliver them from their present bondage and to bring to fulfillment the ancient promises?"[1]

When we were children, one of my brothers would sometimes run to where the rest of us were playing and say, "You have to come home now." Another brother would reply, "Yeah? Well who says so?" If the answer was, "Dad," we knew that name meant something, and it commanded our attention and obedience.

So it was with the Children of Israel. They were not merely inquiring as to the name of the person who claimed to be able to deliver them. They wanted to know if the One who spoke had the authority and power to accomplish that which He promised to do. Because a name has significance, the Israelites wanted to understand that person's name. God responded by revealing something to His people about Himself, just as God reveals Himself to us today through His names. With this understanding in mind, let's take a closer look at God's use of three names in His reply to Moses.

9. Read Exodus 3:14 and 15. Note the different names that God used to reveal Himself (designated by the capitalization of the names).

(a) What was the first name He used (v. 14)?

By this name He was asserting His power to accomplish what He had purposed.

(b) What was the second name He used (v. 15)?

We will learn in lesson 7 that God is personal, the God of redemption, the God of the covenant. By this name, He asserted that He was personally (relationally) interested in the redemption of His people.

(c) What was the third name He used (v. 15)?

We will learn in lesson 3 that this name signifies the God of power, the creator God, the God who can.

The Presence and Power of God

In essence, God was answering Moses' question by saying, "The personal, powerful God of your fathers—the same God who was faithful and powerful on behalf of Abraham and Isaac and Jacob—and who will be faithful to you because of a relationship that exists between us, that's who." By answering the way He did, God was assuring the Children of Israel that the One who had sent Moses to them was the One who could perform the miracle of the exodus.

While this may not be a convincing argument to Americans today, it was *very* reassuring to the Israelites. For the name "I AM" signified the presence and power of God and His willingness to act on their behalf. Speaking of the aspect of the word "presence" implicit in the phrase "I AM THAT I AM," Edward Young wrote: "This presence was an act of grace and not simply the immanent omnipresence of God. The name designates God as present in power."[2] God used this opportunity to say something about Himself; He used a previously unused expression, "I AM." This name took on special significance for the Jewish people, and they remembered it as evidenced by the reaction in Jesus' day when Jesus made the statement, "Before Abraham was, I am" (John 8:58).

10. Read John 8:58 and 59.

(a) What is the connection between the incident recorded in Exodus 3:13–15 and the incident described in John?

(b) What was Jesus claiming, which prompted the Pharisees to want to stone Him?

(c) What is the significance of Christ's statement to believers today?

11. Fifty-one times in the book of Leviticus God began or followed a
    direct command with the statement, "*I am* the LORD [Jehovah]"
    or "*I am* the LORD your God" (italics added). Read Leviticus 11:44;
    18:4, 6, 21; 19:16, 18, 32; 22:31. What is the significance of "I AM"
    in relation to a command?

12. Read the following passages of Scripture. What does the Lord say
    He has done or will do for His people?
    Leviticus 20:8

    Leviticus 22:32

    Isaiah 43:25

    Isaiah 44:24

    Isaiah 48:17

    Isaiah 51:12

    Jeremiah 9:24

It is our human nature to "glory in," or love, being addressed by impressive titles. We tend to give respect and preferential treatment to those who have achieved the emblems of status in our society. We stand in respect when our country's president enters a room. We cease talking when a professor begins class. We respect the conclusions of those bearing the title "doctor," and we esteem very highly the designation CEO. Our human achievements and titles, however, mean nothing in comparison to the name and titles ascribed to God.

13. In Jeremiah 9:23 and 24, God tells us not to glory (or boast) in our wisdom, physical might, or riches. What does God tell us to take pleasure in instead?

14. Read Isaiah 42:8 and then Matthew 23:5–12. What do you believe God wants us to learn from these passages with regard to His name and who He is?

15. How does your knowledge of/relationship with God help you face your trials and difficulties?

CONCLUDING THOUGHTS

Little children sometimes hesitate to do something new or difficult. With pleading eyes they may look to a parent or friend for help. "Will you go with me?" "Will you help me?" With the adult's firm commitment to be present, the child's fears melt away, enabling that child to confidently meet the challenge. Many have said, "If I can be assured that God is leading me, is with me, and will enable me, I will go anywhere and do anything He asks." We are not so different from little children; for we, like them, receive confidence and strength when we are assured that Someone stronger (God) is present and pleased to go with us to help us.

When we face a difficult challenge, we are comforted by God's promises. We take courage by remembering who God is, and how He is ready and willing to work in the lives of His children. Christ's words "I will never leave thee, nor forsake thee" are precious to us (Hebrews 13:5). Like ancient Israel we, too, love to know that the eternal God is our refuge and that underneath us are His everlasting arms (Deuteronomy 33:27). We don't need to pray, "Lord, be with me," for He has promised never to leave us. Instead, we need to remember who God is and pray, "Lord, give me confidence in your Word and make me know the reality of your presence." When we find ourselves hesitant to face life's trials and challenges, may we remember the God who declares, "I AM"; and may each of us be strengthened by His awesome presence and power.

EXPRESS THE TRUTH IN SONG

"Sing forth the honour of his name: make his praise glorious" (Psalm 66:2).

Let's Talk about Jesus
Let's talk about Jesus! The King of kings is He.
The Lord of lords supreme! Throughout eternity.
The great I am the Way, the truth, the Life, the door.
Let's talk about Jesus more and more.
                                                —Buffum Herbert, Jr.

Notes:

1. Edward J. Young, "The Call of Moses-Part II," *Westminster Theological Journal* 30, no. 1, (1967):16.

2. Ibid.

Elohim: God the Powerful

"And said, O LORD God of our fathers, art not thou God in heaven? and rulest not thou over all the kingdoms of the heathen? and in thine hand is there not power and might, so that none is able to withstand thee?" (2 Chronicles 20:6).

Perhaps you can remember when a trial or circumstance looked utterly impossible and you had no idea what to do or where to turn. You might have thought, *I know God can do anything, but can He really make something beautiful out of this mess?* Such experiences aren't reserved for a few tough-skinned super believers—they are something we *all* pass through at one time or another.

No matter where we are in our Christian journey, we can find comfort in knowing that God never allows difficult trials into our lives to destroy us. Rather, He designs them to bring us to realize that *apart from Christ* we can do nothing (John 15:5) and that *with Christ* we can do anything that He wants us to do (Philippians 4:13). God teaches us to rely upon His power rather than on our own willpower, strength, and human ingenuity. Sometimes, the only way for us to learn this lesson is to go through an impossible situation. Whenever God accomplishes the impossible, we become acquainted with Elohim: God the powerful.

STUDY THE WORD

The Power behind Creation

The prophet Jeremiah faced an impossible situation and recognized his inability to turn it around for good. We read in Jeremiah 32:6–27 that the prophet did what many believers have done in the trenches of human experience—he remembered the power of God, and prayed.

1. On what basis did Jeremiah believe God is powerful enough to turn around an impossible situation (Jeremiah 32:17)?

2. First Peter 4:19 tells us that believers can rely upon the Lord to use all of life's trials for good.
    (a) What two words did Peter use to describe God?

    (b) What truths do these two words convey to you?

The very first thing we learn about God in the opening verse of the Bible is that He created the universe and all that is within it. Genesis 1:1 declares that God (Elohim) created heaven and earth. These words give us our first glimpse of God's astounding power and nature, and at the same time, introduce us to the first name mentioned in the Bible—"Elohim." In essence, "Elohim" is a name that represents God the powerful for whom nothing is impossible. So it is fitting that our attention is immediately drawn to God (Elohim), who is powerful enough to have brought the entire creation into existence.

We can be assured that God, who created heaven and earth, is able to sustain and govern His creation. He is able to bring about His perfect will and—at a very personal level—meet all our needs in any situation. Throughout history, multitudes have concluded that since God is powerful enough to have made and sustained the universe, He is able to save any soul, transform any life, work all things together for good in the lives of those who love Him, supply grace to meet any trial, and fulfill every promise He has made.

3. Read Matthew 22:29. According to this verse, what great error did the Pharisees make?

4. Read Psalm 8.
    (a) What statement of praise did David make at the beginning and end of this psalm?

    (b) How did David's contemplation of the solar system and God's creation produce humility in his heart?

5. (a) Read Psalm 33:6–11. By what power did God create the world?

    (b) Read Matthew 8:16. By what means did Jesus heal the sick?

    (c) According to Mark 4:39, by what means did Jesus calm the sea?

6. According to Hebrews 11:3, by what means does God give us the ability to know how the world was created?

'Elohim' and 'elohim'

The name "Elohim" is more a title than a personal name, much like the title "Father" as used by our Lord in the New Testament. For instance, Jesus referred to earthly fathers, yet He also spoke of our Heavenly Father, meaning God. In prayer, He always directly addressed God as "Father." (The only exception was when He prayed on the cross.) Just as the word "father" is used as a description, title, or name, the Hebrew word "elohim" is used in many passages of Scripture in much the same way. The Bible word for God ("Elohim") is also the same word that is used when referring to other gods (other elohim). They are false gods, so they are not really gods at all and have no might, as God has. They are elohim in name only, not in the true sense of being powerful. In contrast, the existence of the living and powerful God is demonstrated in Genesis 1:1 in the creative act of making heaven and earth.

7. Do a quick review of "LORD" from lesson 1 (p. 14) and of "God" from the preceding paragraph. Then fill in the brackets with the Hebrew word from which the English word (in boldface) was translated in Deuteronomy 10:17.

"For the **LORD** [_____] your **God** [_____] is **God** [_____] of **gods** [_____], and Lord of lords, a great God."

God's Power over His Creation

God is the King of Kings and Lord of Lords because God made and owns all creation. The Scriptures tell us that His visible creation reveals His power and, therefore, His authority over all He has made. This is a crucial observation, because failing to recognize God's power leads to a failure to acknowledge God as the rightful owner of everything. This in turn leads to blatant unbelief and a careless disregard for His laws.

8. Read Psalm 19:1–6. What declares the glory of God so plainly that everyone in the world is made aware of His existence and great power?

When the prophets of the Old Testament were about to give God's people an important message from the Lord, they often prefaced it by calling their attention to God's power as seen in His creation. An example can be found in Isaiah 42:5: "Thus saith God the LORD, he that created the heavens" and again in Isaiah 43:1: "But now thus saith the LORD that created thee." By calling the people's attention to God's creative power, the prophets reminded Israel of God's greatness and His worthiness to be heard with humility and submission.

God is invisible to us, but what He has made is plainly visible from the moment we awake in the morning to the moment we fall asleep at night.

9. Read Romans 1:20–25.

    (a) What do we understand about God by observing the visible things He has made (v. 20)?

    (b) What three failures led to what three consequences (vv. 21, 22)?

    (c) Those who acknowledge God's power and authority love and worship Him. What ultimately characterizes those who refuse to recognize the greatness of God's power (v. 25)?

It would be insulting to a great artist for someone to admire his painting and then praise the paint for arranging itself so beautifully on the canvas. It is the artist we credit for the work of art, not the paint. Observing the wonders of God's creation should direct our attention to His worthiness to receive praise from all His creation. Because there is none other who can create heaven and earth or cause it to be inhabited by mankind—there is none other to whom human beings owe respect, obedience, or worship. Elohim is God alone—therefore we owe Him our absolute devotion and worship.

Our Lives, God's Creation

Consider the complexity of a single-cell organism, the precision of our location in the universe, the diversity of species, or the provisions for sustaining life. The perfect balance and timing displayed in God's creation is so mind-boggling that we stand amazed as we ponder it all. God's creation points to a magnificent, intelligent designer and creator. Yet the miracle of salvation is *more* significant than the miracles of creation, for the Bible tells us that the redeemed of the Lord will live forever, long after heaven and earth have passed away. What a comfort to know that *none* of us is too hard for God! He is powerful enough to become our Savior and Redeemer and powerful enough to transform our lives and take us to Heaven for eternity.

10. Read Isaiah 45:18–23. What does God tell us about Himself in these verses?

11. Read Acts 4:10–12; Philippians 2:10; Ephesians 3:9. According to these passages of Scripture, who is the LORD God (Jehovah Elohim) spoken of by Isaiah?

When we imagine we are "an impossible case" and wonder if God can transform our lives to be like Christ's, we have only to remember that the God who feeds the sparrows and makes the sun shine is the same God who delights to create a work of grace in our lives. Believers are a part of God's creation and are meant to be a living display of His great power, just as the beauty of our world displays His power.

12. What does God promise in Philippians 1:6?

13. According to Isaiah 64:8, what does God compare Himself to?

14. How is Christian growth like salvation, according to Galatians 3:2 and 3?

15. Read Hebrews 12:2 and Ephesians 2:10. How does contemplating God's creation of the universe help you believe the truths in these verses?

Elohim's Power Can Be Trusted

At times, life's tragedies and difficulties try our faith and bring us to a place of utter perplexity. Like Job, we try to make sense of things we cannot control and wonder what God is doing and why. Trouble and sorrow make us painfully aware of our human weaknesses and frailties. In the darkness of despair, we have a difficult time understanding how trouble and sorrow can also awaken us to the reality of God's incomprehensible greatness and power.

Job was not different from us. He, too, wanted to understand the reason for his trials—so much so that he imagined that if he could just talk about them face-to-face with God, he would be able to grasp their purpose. Job's faith and understanding of God would not allow him to charge God foolishly, yet Job could not imagine a righteous reason for permitting such tragedy. At Job's lowest point, God gave him his desire and spoke to him out of a whirlwind (Job 38—41), but Job never heard the explanation he was hoping for. Instead, he heard something better.

Job must have been stunned when God began a lengthy series of questions, starting with, "Where wast thou when I laid the foundations of the earth?" (Job 38:4). On and on the questions proceed—through chapters 38, 39, 40, and 41. God never explained the reasons for Job's suffering. He merely pointed out the complexity of His creation and the unexplainable, perfect way He brought it into existence and sustains it. He also pointed out His incomprehensible power. Job became aware of God's power and wisdom in contrast to his own weakness and limited understanding, but he received no explanation for his suffering. As Job considered God's awesome power, his questions melted into silence. In the end, he was content to simply trust Elohim—the extraordinarily powerful creator of the universe—and to this day his trust continues to be abundantly rewarded.

There comes a moment in our lives as believers when we realize that some questions have no answers this side of Heaven. We won't always understand, nor will our prayers and expectations always be answered in the way we would choose. When those times come, we need to remember the explanation given to Job, and simply know that our God is Elohim and can be trusted. Whatever He is doing is good and will eventually reveal His wisdom and great power.

16. What encouraging truths about Elohim do you find in Isaiah 40:25–31?

17. How has God's power miraculously brought good out of a difficult or perplexing event in your life?

CONCLUDING THOUGHTS

Psalm 78 records how God's enemies made a feeble attempt to impugn His ability by asking the question, "Can God furnish a table in the wilderness?" (v. 19). In essence they were saying, 'Yeah, I know that God did thus and so, but can He do this next thing?" Or, "I know that God brought water out of the rock, but I'm not so sure He can bring bread" (see verse 20). The correct response to the skeptic's question, Can God . . . ? is the Scriptural reply, God can. This is the essence of God's name "Elohim."

Can Elohim furnish a table for you and me in the wilderness? Yes, God can! The God who is powerful enough to make and sustain heaven and earth is powerful enough to save us, sustain us, change us, and take us to Heaven. May we say as Moses did, "O Lord GOD, thou hast begun to shew thy servant thy greatness, and thy mighty hand: for what God [Elohim] is there in heaven or in earth, that can do according to thy works, and according to thy might?" (Deuteronomy 3:24).

EXPRESS THE TRUTH IN SONG

"Be thou exalted, LORD, in thine own strength: so will we sing and praise thy power" (Psalm 21:13).

He's Able
He's able, He's able, I know He's able,

I know my Lord is able to carry me thru.
He healed the brokenhearted and He set the captive free.
He made the lame to walk again and He caused the blind to see;
He's able, He's able, I know He's able,
I know my Lord is able to carry me thru.

—Paul Paino

El Elyon: The Most High God

"I will cry unto God most high; unto God that performeth all things for me" (Psalm 57:2).

Every organization has a chain of command with workers ranked in order of importance and power. If someone is engaged in a dispute with a lower-ranking employee, that person might appeal to one who is higher. If the person still isn't satisfied with the judgment, an appeal can be made to the highest-ranking boss, general, CEO, business owner, or court. A person might even get the attention of the president of the United States or NATO's secretary general. But at some point, that person will have appealed to the highest authority and will have no higher authority or power to appeal to—unless, of course, he or she appeals to the most high God.

Both "El Elyon," translated "the most high God," and its shortened form, "Elyon," translated "Most High," speak of God's awesome majesty and supreme position as higher than the highest. The highest-ranking person in the world is nothing before the throne of God. There is no ruler or government or authority over God: God the Most High is the absolute authority. Because God's throne of judgment is the highest governing power in all the heavens and earth, believers are exhorted to call upon the King of Heaven, who is able to change the course of nature or the heart of any person. El Elyon is the final authority in any matter.

STUDY THE WORD

1. What do the following Bible verses say about God's governing authority and its effect on believers?

Proverbs 21:1

2 Corinthians 9:8

2 Peter 2:9

2. (a) Find Psalm 9:1–10 in your Bible and circle the words that
      relate to judging, judgment, or governing.
   (b) David sang joyful praises to El Elyon for His righteous
      judgment. What is the result of knowing God's name, or
      character (v. 10)?

3. Read 1 Peter 2:21–23. Jesus demonstrated how believers are to respond to mistreatment. Jesus did not retaliate in any way when He
   was horribly wronged, but He was not passive. What did He do?

4. God promises to intervene on behalf of those who trust and obey
   Him. What did God say He will do for the believers described in
   each of the following verses?
   Romans 12:18–21

   Exodus 22:22, 23; Deuteronomy 10:17, 18

   1 Thessalonians 4:6

5. Read Psalm 83. Just as Israel today is surrounded by powerful
   enemies, so she was when Asaph wrote this psalm. It may sound as
   if Asaph wanted vengeance, but he did not. Notice the purpose he
   stated in verse 18. What did Asaph want the heathen nations surrounding Israel to know?

Lord of All

The most high God is to be worshiped and honored as He deserves to be. No one is to compete for God's glory and honor or to lift up him- or herself. Rather, the whole world is exhorted to humble itself before the most high God and acknowledge that He is the giver of everything and the highest judge to whom we owe respect. We do not make God lord of our lives, as many suppose. He is Lord over all. We merely come to a place where we are willing to acknowledge His authority and confess that He has the right to govern our lives and expect our submission. We must recognize that God is lifted up and is the Lord of Lords and King of Kings. Ignoring this fact does not diminish God's sovereign authority or power. It merely reveals our foolishness.

6. What did David humbly acknowledge about God in his prayer recorded in 1 Chronicles 29:11–14?

7. Read Psalm 107:8–15.
   (a) Why do some people live satisfied with God's goodness?

   (b) Why does El Elyon humble those who do not recognize His supreme authority?

   (c) Verse 10 tells us that these people live in darkness, enslaved to sin. What causes God to save the afflicted out of their distresses?

   (d) What does this teach you?

8. Read Philippians 2:9–11. What will all the people of the earth do when they admit Jesus is Lord over all?

David began Psalm 145 by acknowledging God as king—King over all kings—with the sovereign right to reign over all creation forever. Read the psalm, noticing how the psalmist praised many attributes, or character qualities, of God and then referred to God's care for His creation and His ability to sustain it. Right in the middle of the psalm (v. 13), David exclaimed that God's kingdom is everlasting and that His dominion endures throughout all generations.

    9. Knowing that God's dominion endures throughout all generations, how should we respond?

The Battle for God's Throne

Lucifer was given great honor and majesty, but he rebelled against God. He did not choose to submit to God's word, but tried to exalt himself to the place of God's dominion. We marvel at Satan's utter arrogance, yet we mimic his attitude when we know God's will and follow our own instead of yielding to God's right to command our obedience. When we ignore God's Word or act contrary to it, we move God off the throne of our hearts and replace the Most High with ourselves. In essence, we do what Satan did and say what he said in his heart.

    10. Read Isaiah 14:12–17.

        (a) How many times did Lucifer (Satan) say, "I will"?

        (b) What is Satan's great ambition?

        (c) What great sin caused Satan to rebel against God's authority?

We love to hear such truths as those that describe God's amazing love toward us. Yet just as important—though less appealing to our human nature—is the truth that El Elyon, the most high God, demands our absolute allegiance and obedience. Because we are self-willed by nature, we naturally rebel against any authority that confronts our wills or thwarts our cherished plans. We don't like yielding our wills or acknowledging

God's right to govern our lives. We'd prefer God merely "be there" to help us accomplish our goals apart from conforming our wills to fit His will.

The Word of God plainly reveals the results of rebellion and submission, and then it grants to mankind the choice to willingly serve El Elyon or self. God is worthy of our worship and obedience. As the most high God, He commands the entire world to bow in reverence to His will and dominion. Those who trust and obey gain great happiness. Those who rebel and refuse to bow will experience great sorrow. It's really just that simple.

11. Read Hosea 7:11–16. In your opinion, why did the people of Ephraim refuse to return to the most high God?

12. Read 1 Peter 5:5.

(a) What character trait is connected to submission to authority?

(b) What character trait is connected to rebellion?

Lessons from a Heathen King

Nebuchadnezzar reigned in Babylon for forty-three years. The Bible has much to say about this prominent heathen king who lived during the days of the prophets Jeremiah, Ezekiel, and Daniel. Many recently discovered documents testify of both his greatness and his arrogance. Nebuchadnezzar is known for the numerous temples and shrines he built to his gods, as well as paved streets, elaborate buildings, and beautiful irrigated gardens. He won many strategic battles and conquered many nations, including the tribe of Judah in the Southern Kingdom.

After a military victory, Nebuchadnezzar often spared the lives of those with a noble lineage and education in order to use their talents and expertise for the benefit of his own kingdom. Daniel was among several young Jewish men who were forcibly taken back to Babylon for this purpose. As a result of his wisdom and God-given ability to interpret the king's dream,

Daniel was elevated to a prominent position in Babylon.

The *International Standard Bible Encyclopedia* says: "The book [Daniel] is not intended to give an account of the life of Daniel. It gives neither his lineage, nor his age, and recounts but a few of the events of his long career. Nor is it meant to give a record of the history of Israel during the exile, nor even of the captivity in Babylon. Its purpose is to show how by His providential guidance, His miraculous interventions, His foreknowledge and almighty power, the God of heaven controls and directs the forces of Nature and the history of nations, the lives of Hebrew captives and of the mightiest of the kings of the earth, for the accomplishment of His Divine and beneficent plans for His servants and people."[1]

Nebuchadnezzar's First Encounter with the Most High God

The king of Babylon encountered the God of Israel when Daniel was able to reveal and interpret the king's dream (Daniel 2). Daniel clearly gave glory to God and told the king the origin of his ruling power (v. 37). Nebuchadnezzar acknowledged God's greater power, but did not submit to Him as the only God worthy of worship and obedience. There was no repentance!

13. Read Daniel 2:37. How did the king of Babylon accomplish great things?

14. Read 1 Corinthians 4:7. How do we accomplish great things?

Nebuchadnezzar's Second Encounter with the Most High God

15. Having refused to bow to the idol that Nebuchadnezzar made, Daniel's three friends were thrown into a furnace. According to Daniel 3:26, who did the king say they were when he saw they were not consumed in the flames?

The king admitted that these men were honorable in worshiping their

God (v. 28), but he still viewed the most high God as the God of the Hebrews, not his God.

Nebuchadnezzar's Third Encounter with the Most High God

Again Daniel was asked to interpret a dream for the king. Daniel told Nebuchadnezzar that the dream revealed that God was going to take the kingdom from him for seven years because of his pride and refusal to repent.

16. What else did God want the king to know and acknowledge (see Daniel 4:25–27, 32)?

17. Daniel implied that Nebuchadnezzar was king only to serve God's purposes and was actually the basest, or lowest, of men (Daniel 4:17). Why do you suppose God would choose to use someone with no real merit or noteworthy qualities to accomplish His will?

In spite of Daniel's revelation, the king insisted on thinking of himself as great and worthy of honor. He said, "Is not this great Babylon, that I have built for the house of the kingdom by the might of my power, and for the honor of my majesty?" (Daniel 4:30).

18. What happened as soon as Nebuchadnezzar spoke these words (see Daniel 4:30–33)?

Nebuchadnezzar's Repentance and Testimony

19. At the end of seven years, the king came to his senses and yielded to God's power and authority. According to Daniel 4:34, what did Nebuchadnezzar then openly acknowledge?

Nebuchadnezzar's Grandson

Belshazzar, Nebuchadnezzar's grandson, knew about all the miraculous encounters his grandfather had had with the most high God, yet he defied God's authority and refused to yield to Him or to repent of his sin. God "crashed his party" when He wrote Belshazzar's destiny on the wall with His hand. Terrified, Belshazzar called for Daniel and asked for an interpretation.

20. Read Daniel 5:18–31.

    (a) For what reason did God remove Nebuchadnezzar from the throne, according to verse 20?

    (b) For what sins was God going to judge Belshazzar (vv. 20–22)?

21. Think about the things you have learned about El Elyon in this lesson. Write an acknowledgment to God that describes who reigns upon the throne of your heart.

CONCLUDING THOUGHTS

God's supreme authority is often ignored even when God Himself is acknowledged. Our failure to honor God's governing authority shows up in many different ways, three of which are common among us. First, we fail to honor God when we forget He is El Elyon, the most high God who presides over the highest court. By failing to commit our "hard cases" to Him for judgment in His time and way, we not only miss seeing God's intervention, but we also miss the joy of seeing Him undertake on our behalf.

Second, we fail to honor God when we forget that He sees every injustice and sin in the heart of every person. When we forget this truth, we do not fear God's certain judgment, heed His warnings, or believe that He truly does respond to every person according to that person's ways. The lack of these things makes us insensitive to that which displeases God, and it invites needless sorrow and chastisement.

Third, we fail to honor God when we forget that everything we have comes from His hand—whether it be our mental or physical abilities, spiritual understanding, or any other blessing we enjoy. In forgetting this truth, we foolishly imagine that we are self-made people. We forget that it is God who ultimately gives us the power to accomplish everything.

As Daniel told Belshazzar, God holds our every breath (Daniel 5:23); He also allows us to make choices. Therefore, we owe God our highest praise and our utmost love and obedience. We are blessed when we come to our senses and surrender our hearts to Him!

EXPRESS THE TRUTH IN SONG

"I will be glad and rejoice in thee: I will sing praise to thy name, O thou most High" (Psalm 9:2).

Come Thou Almighty King

Come, Thou Almighty King,
Help us Thy name to sing,
Help us to praise:
Father all glorious,
O'er all victorious,
Come, and reign over us,
Ancient of Days.

—Anonymous

Note:

1. James Orr, ed. *International Standard Bible Encyclopedia* (Grand Rapids: Eerdmans, 1984), 2:784.

El Roi: God Who Sees Me

*"The eyes of the LORD are upon the righteous, and his ears
are open unto their cry" (Psalm 34:15).*

Somewhere in the world today an expectant mother weeps as she
feels the fluttering kicks of her unborn child. She has been rejected,
abandoned by the child's father, and left to face the future alone.
Her worst nightmare is unfolding in real life, and fear grips her heart. She
struggles to collect her thoughts and whispers as she sobs, "What will I do?
Where will I go? How will I survive? What will happen to my child? Does
anybody care? Does God care? Does He even see what has been done to
me?"

Years ago lived another woman who, like many living today, felt the
lonely pangs of rejection. She, too, wondered what she was going to do and
saw no hope for a bright future. She became pregnant after becoming the
concubine of her barren mistress's husband. This solution to the wife's
infertility was not godly, and reflected the husband and wife's unbelief. You
have probably recognized the couple: Abraham and Sarah.

Sarah eventually admitted that giving her maid Hagar to Abraham
was wrong—but only after Hagar had conceived. Instead of taking respon-
sibility for her sin, Sarah blamed her husband! A confrontation ensued
that ended with Abraham capitulating to Sarah's demands, with disastrous
results.

Caught in the middle of the conflict, feeling used and then rejected by
Sarah, Hagar fled from her home into the harsh desert. She assumed that
no one understood her plight or cared about her welfare. The Bible tells
us that the Angel of the Lord (the preincarnate Christ) found Hagar by a
spring of water and spoke to her there.

STUDY THE WORD

1. Read Genesis 16:8–12.

   (a) What two questions did the Lord ask Hagar?

   (b) What did the Lord tell Hagar to do (v. 9)?

   (c) What did the Lord promise (v. 10)?

   (d) What did the Lord tell Hagar about her unborn child (v. 11)?

   (e) Why did the Lord tell Hagar to name her son "Ishmael," meaning "God will hear" (v. 11)?

Hagar's sorrow turned to hope when she realized that someone did understand and did care. She was moved with awe at the realization that God saw her plight and knew all about her heartaches and difficulties. Hagar learned a life-changing truth about God in that lonely desert place: He sees everything, but more specifically, He sees "me."

2. Read Genesis 16:13 and 14.

   (a) What name did Hagar call the Lord?

   (b) Using a study Bible, a concordance, or a Hebrew lexicon, find the word *Beer Lahai Roi,* which is the name Hagar gave to the well where she met God. (It can also be spelled as one word or with hyphens between the parts.) What does it mean?

   (c) What is the significance of this name?

3. When we experience heartaches, God is present to guide and comfort us. What concern or sorrow does God see in your heart right now?

Doesn't Anyone Care?

King David endured many conflicts and sorrows. He, like Hagar, came to a time when he felt overwhelmed with grief and believed that no one understood or cared about him. Alone in a cave and filled with despair, he cried to the Lord and poured out all his troubles. God heard David's cry and spoke to his heart with comforting truths, causing David to regain hope in God's promises and faithfulness. David concluded that God knew all about his trouble and cared for him.

4. Read Psalm 142.

(a) What did David declare he believed (v. 5)?

(b) What did David request (vv. 6, 7)?

(c) How did David's response follow the eternal principles that are recorded in Philippians 4:6 and 7?

(d) What encouraging truth concludes David's song?

Jesus Loves Even Me

It is one thing to know that God loves the world, but it is quite another to know God loves "me." As Christians, we know that God is everywhere and sees everything. We can sing of His love and omnipresence with the crowd and easily believe God is aware of our corporate efforts to love and serve Him. Yet in spite of what we know, we have a hard time comprehending that God knows each of us intimately and understands us perfectly, as no one else can. We easily forget that God is present with us always, seeing and hearing our every thought, word, and action. Perhaps we have such difficulty because knowing that God can see everything is not the same as knowing that God sees "me."

Before we will know the joy of God's presence, we must come to the point when our hearts, not our heads, are convinced that our God is a personal God. We must be able to say with absolute confidence, "He knows me. He loves me. He sees me." The human heart longs for tangible proof of this fact—proof that we can see, touch, or feel. But God wants us to believe what He declares to be true in His Word. He wants us to live by faith, not by "feel."

Psalm 139 is a personal, beautiful acknowledgment that God made, knows, and sees every individual. David rejoiced in the exhilarating realization that God understood every quirky little thing there was to know about him. David was awed to know that he could never be out of God's sight, that even in his mother's womb, God saw him and formed him. By the end of his song, David could hardly contain his praise, thankfulness, and joy.

5. Read Psalm 139, applying it to yourself every time you come to the word "me." What are you glad God knows about you?

6. God sees the littlest details surrounding every living creature. After reading Matthew 10:29 and 30, describe what you believe these verses reveal about our God.

God Sees Those Who Trust Him

King Asa began his reign eager to obey and serve the Lord. As a result, God abundantly blessed the nation of Judah. When Asa was faced with an invading army of Ethiopians greatly outnumbering his own army, he cried to the Lord: "Lord, it is nothing with thee to help, whether with many, or with them that have no power: help us, O Lord our God; for we rest on thee, and in thy name we go against this multitude. O Lord, thou art our God; let not man prevail against thee" (2 Chronicles 14:11). Asa believed that God saw his predicament, so he relied upon Him for deliverance. As a result, he was given a fabulous victory over the Ethiopians. Asa zealously renewed his commitment to obey and seek the Lord, and again God blessed him.

Thirty-five years went by, during which time Asa learned to rely upon his own reasoning rather than on the Lord. When the Northern Kingdom (Israel) threatened to cut off his trade routes, rather than turning to the Lord, Asa turned to the king of Syria. Together they devised a battle strategy that succeeded in destroying Israel's plans. Shortly thereafter, however, the man of God confronted Asa with his error.

    7. Read 2 Chronicles 16:1–8.

       (a) What did the prophet say was the reason Asa had victory over the Ethiopians (v. 8)?

       (b) God looks for those who believe that He sees them and who rely upon Him wholeheartedly. What does verse 9 say He will do for such people?

God Sees Those Who Fear Him

As little children, my siblings and I often found comfort knowing our mother was close by keeping her "eye" on us. If we got ourselves into difficulty, we had only to call, and Mom was quickly there, ready to defend, help, or console us. Of course, the fact that she was "keeping her eye" on us also meant that she was aware when we willfully chose to disobey or act unruly. Her presence was both a comfort and a deterrent when we were tempted to do wrong. We feared Mom in the sense that we feared the certain consequences of disobedience. We also feared Mom in the sense that we had respect for her authority as well as her love. As a result, we trusted her care for us and felt secure in her watchfulness over us.

The Bible tells us that "the eye of the LORD is upon them that fear him" (Psalm 33:18). Our Heavenly Father "keeps His eye" on those who fear Him, and is ready to defend, help, and comfort them in any trouble. He is also ready to discipline and guide His children away from sin and its devastations. The more we know this and are aware of God's presence and shepherding care, the more we learn to properly fear Him. As a result, we obtain many blessings and find great security in the watchful care of our loving Heavenly Father.

    8. God's watchful eye is one benefit of fearing God. Write the benefits of fearing God that are found in each of the following verses.
       Psalm 34:9

       Psalm 103:11

       Psalm 115:11

       Psalm 145:19

       Proverbs 9:10

       Proverbs 14:26

       Proverbs 14:27

God Sees Our Tears

    Some people have hearts so cold and indifferent that they are unmoved by tears of suffering. They oppress others and ignore the tears of those whom they mistreat. Solomon lamented in Ecclesiastes 4:1 that the oppressed often have no one to comfort them. From the world's point of view, this is a rather gloomy picture. However, from a Christian's perspective, the picture looks quite different. Believers have an advocate in Heaven who sees and undertakes for them. There is a comforter, and there is someone who sees and cares. What a comfort to read, "The eyes of the LORD are upon the righteous, and his ears are open unto their cry" (Psalm 34:15).

    9. Psalm 34 describes how the Lord meticulously cares for believers, seeing when we are in trouble, hearing when we cry, and being ready to comfort and deliver us out of every affliction.
    (a) Read Psalm 34, circling the word "all" each time you find it.

(b) What "all" does God see and deliver us from when we put our trust in Him?

10. Read Deuteronomy 26:7–9 and Isaiah 38:5 to discover what God saw that moved Him to respond. What was it?

God Sees Everything

Many people profess that they believe in God. But they have not had a change of heart (repentance) toward God, nor have they put their trust in Christ for forgiveness of their sins. These people acknowledge God's existence but do not believe that God is observing their behavior or holding them responsible for their sins. They do not fear God's judgment, because they do not believe that He takes note of them.

11. Read Psalm 94:7–11. What did the psalmist call those who think God does not see them?

Human beings tend to behave differently when they believe they are not being observed or believe they can sin with impunity. A fifth-grade teacher announced to her class that she would be leaving the classroom for ten minutes. She carefully instructed the class to quietly read their textbooks while she ran an errand, and then she walked out of the room. Do you suppose every child did as the class had been told? Or would you guess that the children began to whisper, giggle, and move about the room? If you guessed that the majority of the students took advantage of the situation, you guessed correctly. The children misbehaved because they had no fear the teacher would see or discipline them. Only when someone whispered, "She's coming!" did the class become quiet and studiously resume reading their books.

Some of us might be "smarter than a fifth grader," but we are very much like one when we imagine that God is absent or does not see us or hold us responsible for our disobedience. Just as the fifth graders did not

fear the teacher, so we do not fear God if we believe He is occupied else-
where. Our Christian lives mature when we develop an awareness of God's
presence. With that awareness comes the certain knowledge that, indeed,
He does see and know everything we think, say, and do, just as He knows
everything that others think, say, and do. Our behavior reflects what we
believe. When we are convinced that "the eyes of the LORD are in every
place, beholding the evil and the good" (Proverbs 15:3), we will more easily adjust our own behavior as well as trust God to deal with the behavior
of others.

    12. Read Jeremiah 23:23 and 24. What do these verses teach about
        hiding from God?

    13. Read Hebrews 4:13. What does this verse say about God's ability to
        see everything?

God Sees When We Do Well

    People do not always notice when we make a sacrifice on behalf of
others or when we do well. Our greatest acts of kindness might be unseen
by others, while the depth of our love for Christ can be overlooked as well.
It is not humanly possible for another human being to see what only God
can see, nor is it in our human nature to be flawlessly concerned about
the efforts of others. We are limited and imperfect in our ability to judge
righteously—but God is not. He sees every act of kindness and knows every
motive and effort underlying it.

    14. Read Hebrews 6:10. What labor of love does God promise to see
        and remember that people may forget?

    Although many Christians say they believe that God sees and rewards
all that is done for His name's sake, they sometimes act as though He does
not. These people draw attention to themselves whenever they can so that

others will be aware of their good deeds. They are not content to know that God sees what they do. In Matthew 6:5 and 6, Jesus warned about this kind of outwardly "good" behavior. He gave a name to those who pray and serve to be seen by people: "hypocrites." These spiritual pretenders serve their own appetites for praise; they do not serve God.

15. Jesus told us that our Heavenly Father sees what we do in secret. What will He do for those who pray and give without regard for who sees?

16. How does this promise relate to the promise found in James 4:10?

17. Read Deuteronomy 6:18. What does God promise to those who do what is right and good in His sight?

CONCLUDING THOUGHTS

To know that God sees and cares about us personally changes the way we live. Most importantly, it is a pivotal truth that has the power to transform hopelessness and despair into confidence and peace. If God sees and cares, He will also undertake for us and mercifully sustain us in our darkest hours and deepest disappointments.

Hagar was deeply touched when she realized that the all-powerful God of creation not only knew her name and her problems, but had solutions for them as well. When she called the Lord El Roi—the God who sees me—she was expressing more than a belief that God sees what goes on in the world. She was expressing the deep conviction that God knew her personally and took an active interest in her life. May each one of us come to know the tender love and care of El Roi, and be comforted in the realization that truly "He sees me."

EXPRESS THE TRUTH IN SONG

"Praise the Lord; for the Lord is good: sing praises unto his name; for it is pleasant" (Psalm 135:3).

Commit and Trust

Commit thy way unto the Lord.
All you need He will afford.
Never fret or be oppressed.
Commit and trust, delight and rest.

Trust in Him, His Word is true.
He will do what's right for you.
Praise the Name you have confessed.
Commit and trust, delight and rest.

Chorus

Fret not! He's watching over you
Fret not! The Lord will see you thro'
Fret not! You're sure to stand the test,
Commit and trust, delight and rest.

—Bill Harvey

El Shaddai: Almighty God

"He that dwelleth in the secret place of the most High shall abide under the shadow of the Almighty" (Psalm 91:1).

Imagine the disappointment of John, a professional mountain climber who trained for years to climb the world's highest peak, but before he reached the top, he collapsed, exhausted. He had expended all his strength and endurance, and had to turn back.

Can you feel the pain of Tad and Brenda, a young couple who saved and planned so they could purchase their first home? When at last they found their dream home, they were turned away because they did not qualify for a loan.

Or envision the deep disappointment of Carol, a recent graduate who studied hard to pass the board exams to become a registered nurse. Just weeks before the exam, she was hit by a drunk driver and sustained a major head injury. Though she recovered to a point, she was unable to regain enough mental capacity to pass her exams.

These four people had limited resources to do what they deeply desired to do. Like all human beings, no matter how much they had, they were limited in their strength, wealth, mental capacity, or talent. The best doctor in the world cannot keep his wealthiest terminally ill patient alive, and no one has the power to save his or her own soul. A human being may be powerful, but not one of us is all-powerful, and not one has unlimited resources. All of us have a finite amount of everything, no matter how hard we work or how great our desire. Only one person has unlimited resources and power, and that is God Almighty: El Shaddai.

The Hebrew word *Shaddai* refers to the unlimited nature of God's power and resources, or, as Paul described it, the "unsearchable riches of

Christ" (Ephesians 3:8) or the "exceeding riches of his grace" (2:7).

Whenever the prefix "El" (short for "Elohim") appears in front of a Hebrew name, it refers to God, the powerful. So "El Shaddai" emphasizes God's unlimited resources and inexhaustible grace, love, and mercy.

Unlike us, God cannot be more of anything or have less of anything. Everything He is or has is infinite. God has *all* power and is *all* sufficient in *every* way. He is able to fulfill any promise, no matter how impossible it may seem, for there is absolutely nothing impossible to God. He is God Almighty: El Shaddai.

STUDY THE WORD

Blessings for God's People

God introduced His name "El Shaddai" in Genesis 17:1. God appeared to Abram and said to him, "I am the Almighty God; walk before me, and be thou perfect [mature, blameless]." Immediately following this pronouncement, God gave Abram several gracious promises.

1. List the promises made to Abram/Abraham (vv. 2–8).

2. Why do you believe that God prefaced these promises by stating His name "El Shaddai"?

When Sarah overheard the Lord telling Abraham that she was going to have a baby, she laughed to herself. It struck her funny, since she knew it would be impossible for a ninety-year-old woman who was well past menopause to conceive a child. She greatly underestimated God's power as well as God's willingness and ability to bless her beyond the realm of human possibility and to fulfill His promise to Abraham. Knowing Sarah's secret thoughts, the Lord challenged her inward chuckle of disbelief.

3. (a) What question did the Lord ask that caused Sarah to react with fear? See Genesis 18:11–15.

(b) What do you believe caused Sarah to be afraid?

The next time the name "God Almighty" appears in the Bible is in Genesis 28:3. Isaac gave Jacob instructions to go to a faraway place called Padanaram to find a wife. Isaac asked that God Almighty would bless Jacob. By using the name "El Shaddai," a Hebrew would be reminded that God (Elohim) had an unlimited supply of gracious blessings for His people. In essence, Isaac was emphasizing God's power in relation to His bountiful, infinite blessings.

    4. Read Genesis 28:3 and 4. What similarities are there between Isaac's statements to Jacob and the statements God gave to Abraham as recorded in Genesis 17:1–8?

    5. Read Genesis 43:14, 48:3, and 49:25, which use "God Almighty." What theme is revealed through the repeated words?

The Heritage of God's People

Every child of God has a heritage or inheritance that is his or hers simply because that person has been redeemed and belongs to God. Just as Almighty God made a covenant with Abraham that secured specific blessings, or promises, so He makes a covenant with us as believers at the moment of our salvation.

    6. Read Revelation 1:6–18. Who was speaking (vv. 8, 11, 17, 18), and whom did John identify as the "Almighty" (v. 8)?

The desire for a perfect, loving father lives in the corner of every child's heart. Earthly fathers sometimes fail us, but our perfect Heavenly Father never abandons or forsakes His own. The Bible tells us that the Lord

Almighty promises to be a father to us (2 Corinthians 6:18). God invites His children to draw close to Him and share the joys of an intimate father-child relationship.

    7. Read 2 Corinthians 6:14–18. What does God require of His children so they may share this kind of fellowship with Him?

When a person believes on the Lord Jesus Christ, that person enters into a binding, eternal covenant with God. At that moment, the believer is irrevocably born into God's family. God will deal with that believer as a father deals with his own child, not as someone would deal with an enemy or stranger. God promises to give all of His children access to His throne, eternal life, forgiveness of sins, and a future home in Heaven—among many other blessings. He promises He will discipline His rebellious children yet be ready to immediately restore full fellowship when they repent. These are just a few of the precious privileges that are the heritage of every believer.

Many blessings are given to God's children unconditionally, meaning God will fulfill His promise whether His child is obedient or disobedient. Listed below are several verses of Scripture, each containing an unconditional promise that God gives to believers.

    8. Write the promise found in each of the following verses.

      Psalm 46:1

      Psalm 147:3

      Matthew 28:20

      John 3:16

John 6:40

John 10:28, 29

Romans 8:38, 39

1 Corinthians 10:13

Ephesians 1:3

1 Thessalonians 4:16, 17

God has given many conditional promises. He fulfills these promises only when the believer fulfills his or her part.

    9. Listed below are sixteen verses containing a *conditional* promise. For each verse or passage, write both the believer's responsibility and God's promise.

Passage	*Believer's Responsibility (the condition)*	*God's Promise*
Matthew 7:7		
Galatians 5:16		
Galatians 6:9		
Philippians 4:6, 7		

Passage	Believer's Responsibility (the condition)	God's Promise
Colossians 3:23, 24		
James 4:10		
2 Peter 1:2–4		

The Problem of Unbelief

The unsaved struggle to believe that an all-powerful God exists. They cannot accept that He not only has the power to have created the world in six days but that He has the power to have fulfilled every miracle mentioned in the Bible, including granting eternal life to repentant sinners. They tend to conclude that if these things are impossible for people to do, they are not possible at all. Consulting with God or drawing upon His abundant resources is not a consideration for them. In fact, the absence of God in their thinking causes them to view the believer's confidence in God with disdain. They live believing they are sufficient to meet their own needs, rather than believing that God is sufficient to meet every need.

In the opinion of those who have not trusted Christ for salvation, the idea that God is a present, personal God whose love and grace have no limit and who delights to fulfill His promises is an incredible, if not presumptuous, claim. Unbelievers do not know or understand Almighty God, who fulfills every impossible promise given to His children when they trust Him to do what He said He would do. The very thought that such a God exists is inconceivable to those who refuse to believe God's Word. Yet a believer who gets a clear glimpse of God's divine nature has no trouble believing the miracles of the Bible or God's promises. The discovery of God's promises and the realization that God delights to fulfill His Word thrills and comforts His children.

    10. Read 1 Corinthians 2:9 and Psalm 68:19. What do the promises in these verses cause you to believe about God?

God of the Impossible

The angel Gabriel visited a faithful priest named Zacharias to an-nounce the coming birth of a son to him and his wife, Elisabeth. Because they were old and the fulfillment of the promise a human impossibility, Zacharias challenged the message Gabriel brought from God.

11. Read Luke 1:5–20. For what reason did the angel make Zacharias mute?

Six months later, Gabriel visited Mary, a young woman engaged to be married. The angel brought her, too, a message from God, explaining that she was going to give birth to the promised Messiah.

12. Read Luke 1:26–38. How was Mary's response different from Zach-arias's?

13. Mary was young and limited in her knowledge of spiritual things, while Zacharias was old and knowledgeable concerning the Scrip-tures and the promises of God. What do you believe made the dif-ference in the way they responded to the angel's message?

We often remember Martha as the perfectionist sister who was too busy to sit with her more spiritually minded sister at the Savior's feet. Yet we overlook Martha's spiritual understanding and faith when we fail to see the significance of other events that shed light on her character.

14. Read John 11:20–28.

    (a) Mary and Martha each chose a different response as Jesus ap-proached their home. What did each of them do?

    (b) In verse 22, what was Martha stating that she believed?

(c) What impossible promises did Christ tell Martha He would fulfill (vv. 23–26)?

(d) Do you think Martha believed Jesus was going to immediately
raise her brother from the dead? Why or why not?

CONCLUDING THOUGHTS

As we begin to comprehend the full meaning of the name "El Shaddai," we develop confidence in God's willingness and ability to fulfill His
promises. For instance, we know that He will forgive us because He has
promised to forgive all who confess and forsake their sin (1 John 1:9).
We do not fear that God's patience will run out or that His mercy will be
exhausted, because we understand that our God has enough patience and
mercy to meet any need and to forgive all our sin (Psalm 86:5).

We do not keep our distance from God's throne when we pray, afraid
we've talked too much, asked too much, or taken up too much of God's
time. When we know that God Almighty invites us to come boldly to His
throne to find mercy and grace for every need, we are filled with hope and
confidence (Hebrews 4:16). We gladly come on the basis of His promises
and goodness, rather than on our good works or perfection.

We are able to face life's trials without anxiety and dread because we
know that God has promised to give sufficient grace to meet any difficulty
(2 Corinthians 12:9). We don't fear we've used up all of God's blessings,
or exhausted His willingness to help, or exceeded the number of promises
He will fulfill on our behalf (Philippians 4:19). The only thing that limits
what we receive from God is us. His Word says that He has provided all
we need to live happy, godly, and blessed lives and has given us exceeding
great and precious promises that enable us to be like Him (2 Peter 1:2–4).

When our human resources fail us—and they will fail us—and when
we come to a place where God is all we have, we will find that He is all we
need. It has been said that man's extremity is God's opportunity. Every

child of God who has learned how to claim God's promises has found this
to be true. Sarah and Abraham, Martha, Elisabeth, and Mary all testify to
this truth. We are able to depend on God in every situation because He is
all-powerful, sufficient, and infinitely gracious. He never sleeps, never fails,
and never grows weary with our human frailties. There is nothing too hard
for our God, for He is El Shaddai—God Almighty.

EXPRESS THE TRUTH IN SONG

"And they sing the song of Moses the servant of God, and the song of
the Lamb, saying, Great and marvellous are thy works, Lord God Almighty;
just and true are thy ways, thou King of saints" (Revelation 15:3).

He Giveth More Grace
He giveth more grace when the burdens grow greater.
He sendeth more strength when the labors increase;
To added affliction He addeth His mercy,
To multiplied trials, His multiplied peace.

When we have exhausted our store of endurance,
When our strength has failed ere the day is half done,
When we reach the end of our hoarded resources,
Our Father's full giving is only begun.

Chorus
His love has no limit; His grace has no measure,
His power has no boundary known unto men;
For out of His infinite riches in Jesus,
He giveth, and giveth, and giveth again!

—Annie Johnson Flint

Jehovah: The Lord My God

"Trust ye in the LORD for ever: for in the LORD Jehovah is everlasting strength" (Isaiah 26:4).

The president of the United States has several titles that express the nature of his position. He is, for example, the Commander in Chief, meaning he is the top-ranking commander of the United States military. Similarly, he is properly addressed as "Mr. President" when he is being spoken to by the press or others. He might also be referred to as the "head of state," meaning he is the chief public representative of our nation. And it is customary to announce the arrival of "the President of the United States of America" when he enters a room. There are many presidents, but only one is currently the "president of the United States." Hence, this designation is appropriate to distinguish him from others.

All of these titles have a specific meaning and give us a more complete understanding of the president's role. His first name, however, is used in a completely different way. Unless one knew him personally, it would be disrespectful to address the presiding president of the United States by using his first name. Only those who know him, such as his own family and friends, use his personal name and address him with it.

No matter where you are in life, you also have names and titles that express who you are: valedictorian, Employee of the Month, customer service representative, Mrs. or Miss or Ms., CEO, Your Honor, Officer, or (fill in the blank) _____. These titles have their place, but when you become personally acquainted with another person, you often invite that person to drop the title and use your personal or first name.

When we study the name "Jehovah," it is important to understand that we are discussing God's personal proper name, not His title. It is a name that was not normally used in Old Testament times by anyone other than His people, and it refers to no other than the one and only Lord God. This fact gives us our first clue as to the significance of the name "Jehovah," for it is the sacred personal name of God, who seeks a personal relationship with His own. This name embodies not only who He is, but also all that He is to each believer.

STUDY THE WORD

1. Read 2 Kings 1:2. What was the personal name of the god of Ekron?

Name Above All Names

In the Old Testament, "JEHOVAH" is usually translated either "GOD" or "LORD" and is printed in capital letters to signify reverence and great respect. "JEHOVAH" is actually a transliteration of the Hebrew name YHWH. It originated with Christians living in the Middle Ages.

The Hebrew people so honored the personal name of God that they refused to pronounce it out loud or even write it in its entirety. Because the name was not spoken aloud by the Jewish people, the correct pronunciation of YHWH was lost during the time that the Jews returned from exile. Scholars today believe that YHWH would be pronounced YAHWEH, but no one knows for sure what the original pronunciation was. JEHOVAH is the traditional pronunciation, so that is what we will use in this lesson.

As the sanctity of God's personal name became increasingly more important to the Hebrew people, they expressed their desire to avoid its misuse or treat it lightly by reading the name "YHWH" as "Adonai," the Hebrew word for "Lord." The scribes further expressed reverence for God's name by washing their pens and bathing before they wrote it. While the Jewish rituals connected with God's name and the refusal to speak His name aloud weren't prescribed by God, the Jews' efforts are a tribute to their reverence for His name.

2. The Bible has much to say about the honor of God's name; therefore, Israel's zeal ought to provoke us to examine the depth of our
own reverence for the name of God. What word in each verse describes the way we should regard God's name?

Psalm 148:13—God's name is _____ .

Psalm 145:21—God's name is _____ .

Psalm 72:19—God's name is_____ .

Psalm 66:2—God's name is _____ .

When God gave Moses His law, He included, "Thou shalt not take the
name of the LORD thy God in vain" (Exodus 20:7). This is the command-
ment that motivated Israel to use great care in the way they thought of or
used God's name. The Hebrew people concluded they would never violate
this command if they never said God's name out loud. They erred by not
realizing that it is heartfelt reverence for God's name, not avoidance of His
name, that God desires.

A person might misuse the name of the Lord in many ways. Using the
Lord's name in a joke treats it lightly and reveals a lack of reverence. When
we make a promise or vow in God's name and do not keep it, we bring disapproval upon our God and misuse His name. People who use God's name
when they curse and swear abuse the Lord's name by incorporating it into
the vilest of human expressions. Even using the common expression, "Oh,
my God!" treats the Lord's name in an irreverent, flippant way and makes
it a common expression that has nothing to do with God's honor or with
love for God. These are just a few of the many ways both Christians and
unbelievers make light of God's name and fail to treat it as a sacred name
that is worthy of honor and utmost respect.

3. Read Deuteronomy 5:11. How will God respond to those who misuse His name and treat it lightly?

4. According to the following verses, who takes God's name in vain?
   Psalm 139:20

   Psalm 74:10

5. According to the following verses, who honors God's name?
   Psalm 89:7

   Psalm 111:9

6. What are some ways you can honor God's name throughout each
   day?

The Lord, My God

The personal name of God, "Jehovah," occurs in the Bible over 5,500
times. In Psalms, the original (Hebrew) is sometimes contracted to "JAH,"
which is the concluding syllable of "hallelujah" and "Elijah," for example.
"Jehovah" is more fully defined in Scripture than any other name or title
referring to God. In addition to various other meanings, the name "Jehovah" exhibits the innermost depths of the divine Being and the personal
nature of God. He is Jehovah, "the self-existing One," but more specifically,
He is Jehovah, the personal God of those who love and obey Him.

7. Read Exodus 6:3. What name of God did Abraham, Isaac, and
   Jacob know and understand?

The name "Jehovah" does not appear in the Scriptures until Exodus 6.
Many scholars believe that God did not introduce this name until then
because He wanted to emphasize that, for the first time, the nation of Israel
was going to have a personal relationship with Him. Although Abraham,
Isaac, and Jacob had known the name "Jehovah," they did not know its
meaning or significance. Moses was the first to know the character of

"Jehovah" as a personal God; whereas prior to Moses, people knew the name "Jehovah" as "THE God" rather than as their personal God.

    8. Read Exodus 6:7. What statement indicates that God wanted the Israelites to know that He was their personal God?

The Lord, My Redeemer

    9. Jehovah Himself imparted to Moses the meaning of His personal name. Read Exodus 34:5–7. List the character descriptions that God ascribed to Himself that are represented in the name "Jehovah."

Notice that the last half of verse 7 speaks of God's justice. Those who do not come to God in humility, seeking His mercy and forgiveness, will receive a just recompense for their sin.

    10. What character quality compelled the Son of God to come to earth and die on the cross for our sins? (See 1 Peter 3:18 and John 3:16 and 17.)

Mercy is extended to people today on the same basis that it was offered to Israel—not because we deserve it, but because it is part of God's divine character. The Bible tells us that it is by grace that we are saved, through faith, not by our own efforts.

    11. Read Ephesians 2:8 and 9. What statement helps us understand that redemption cost Christ dearly but does not cost those He redeems (saves)?

We can remember the difference between grace and mercy by recalling that grace gives us what we do not deserve, while mercy withholds from us what we do deserve. Because God is merciful, He took upon Himself the just penalty for our sin. This is the basis for our redemption.

The divine attributes that play a part in the story of Israel's redemption from Egypt, as well as our redemption from the penalty of sin, are holiness, justice, and love for sinners. We typically see the name "Jehovah" used in connection with Israel's redemption because the name represents all of the attributes involved in the Israelites' personal relationship with God as their redeemer. The name "Jehovah" appears where relationships between God and people are involved, and especially when speaking of redemption in some way.

12. Read Exodus 6:6 and Colossians 1:13. How is the redemption of Israel like the redemption of believers?

The LORD, My Guarantor

13. Look up the word "guarantee" in a dictionary. Write the definition.

14. Look up the word "covenant" in a dictionary. Write the definition.

A guarantor is one who makes or gives a guarantee. Jehovah gave His people a guarantee that He will fulfill the covenant He made with them. Whenever the Scriptures speak of the covenant relationship between God and man, it uses the name "Jehovah."

15. In your Bible, circle the word "I" each time it occurs in Exodus 6:8. Then, below write the word or words that follow each "I" in the verse.

I _____ .

I _____ .

I _____ .

I _____ .

16. Jehovah, our God, guarantees He will fulfill His promises to His
own. Read each of the following passages of Scripture. Identify with
whom God made a covenant and *what* He promised to do.

Passage	Who	What
Genesis 2:16, 17		
Genesis 12:1–3		
Genesis 15:2–5		
Genesis 28:13–15		
Exodus 6:7		
Deuteronomy 29:1, 10–15		
1 Chronicles 17:11–13; 2 Chronicles 6:16		

17. Read Isaiah 48:17.

(a) What words emphasize the idea that Jehovah is a personal God?

(b) What word speaks of Jehovah as Savior?

(c) What words describe what Jehovah does on the personal behalf
of each believer?

The name "Jehovah" is not used in the New Testament, because Jesus
is the embodiment of all that Jehovah was to His people.
18. Read Isaiah 44:6.
(a) Who is "the LORD of hosts"?

(b) Why do you believe this?

19. Although the name "Jesus" is not used in the Old Testament, we
know that Jesus Christ is described and revealed to us throughout
the Old Testament Scriptures. How do we know this, according to
Luke 24:27 and 44–47?

CONCLUDING THOUGHTS

The name "Jehovah" is one of the more fascinating names of God,
shrouded in some mystery but revealing His character and nature. One of
the most important facts to remember about the name "Jehovah" is that
the Bible used it in the context of His personal relationship to Israel. It is
most often used (1) when speaking of His work on behalf of His people
Israel; (2) when speaking of His special relationship as redeemer of Israel;
and (3) when speaking of His covenantal promises and relationship with
the Israelites or Jews.

The name "Elohim" (printed "God" in our English Bibles) is plural in
its form and suggests the fact of three Persons, while the name "Adonai"
(printed "Lord") proclaims divine authority. Both "Elohim" and "Adonai"
are less distinctive than the name "Jehovah," since these titles are sometimes ascribed to creatures or people. "Jehovah" is unique, because it is the

proper name of the one true God and is not shared by anyone or anything else. "Elohim" represents God the powerful, the God who can; but "Jehovah" represents God the personal, the God who acts for "me." Thus He is Jehovah, the Elohim of all who put their trust in Him. It is amazing that the magnificent God of the Old Testament is the same God we serve today. He wants to be our personal God and not just a name we read in the Bible or sing about in church. Jehovah is whispering for you to draw near to Him and know him intimately.

EXPRESS THE TRUTH IN SONG

"Sing unto God, sing praises to his name: extol him that rideth upon the heavens by his name JAH, and rejoice before him" (Psalm 68:4).

Now with Joyful Exultation
Now with joyful exultation
Let us sing Jehovah's praise,
To the rock of our salvation
Loud hosannas let us raise.
Thankful tribute gladly bringing,
Let us come before Him now,
And with psalms His praises singing,
Joyful in His presence bow.

For how great a God, and glorious,
Is Jehovah whom we sing;
Over idol gods victorious,
Great is He, our God and King.
In His hand are earth's deep places,
His the strength of all the hills,
His the sea whose bounds He traces,
His the land His bounty fills.
                                        —John Zendel

Jehovah-Shalom: God Our Peace

"For unto us a child is born, unto us a son is given: and the government shall be upon his shoulder: and his name shall be called Wonderful, Counsellor, The mighty God, The everlasting Father, The Prince of Peace" (Isaiah 9:6).

To be at peace is to be at rest, free from strife, worry, or discontent. No wonder every human being in every nation and in every age—whether rich or poor, old or young—seeks to experience it. Yet peace is never found by seeking for it. It cannot be bought, nor can it be acquired by one's skill or dedication to achieving it. It is found only when people meet the God of peace, Jehovah-Shalom.

During the time of the judges, Israel went through several sin cycles, resulting in the consequences of sin, repentance, and then deliverance by God. Israel's experience pictures the often-tumultuous spiritual life of believers. When we believers ignore the Lord and follow our own ways, we often forfeit our peace and joy. But when we call upon God in repentance, the Lord hears our cries, strengthens us, and blesses us with peace (Psalm 29:11). The birthright of every believer is to know Jehovah-Shalom!

In a cycle of oppression by the Midianites, Israel began to cry out to the Lord. In answer, God began to deliver them from their afflictions, but He did so in ways they would not have imagined.

STUDY THE WORD

1. Read Judges 6:11–13. The angel of the Lord sat under an oak tree and then began to speak to Gideon.

(a) How did the Lord greet Gideon?

(b) What did Gideon immediately ask after he heard the words, "The LORD is with thee"?

(c) Have you ever asked why certain things were happening? Do you believe it is wrong to ask why? Explain.

2. Read Judges 6:14–24. The Lord told Gideon to save Israel out of the hand of the Midianites, but Gideon had no peace in his heart upon hearing these words.
    (a) What two things did the Lord say, similar to His opening greeting, to assure Gideon that he would succeed?

    (b) What reason did Gideon give for his fear?

    (c) When Gideon realized he had been talking to the Lord, he feared he would die. What did the Lord say to comfort him?

    (d) Gideon built an altar to the Lord and called it Jehovah-Shalom. Why do you believe Gideon chose this name?

3. What kind of thoughts and desires does the Lord have toward His people? (Jeremiah 29:11).

4. Who is being referred to as "The Prince of Peace" in Isaiah 9:6?

Peace with God

Having peace with God and knowing the peace of God are two separate

things. Peace with God refers to our reconciliation with, or relationship
to, God, while the peace of God refers to the practical outcome of our faith
and dependence upon Christ. Those who rest in the promises and character
of a faithful God have perfect peace. It is theirs alone.

The Bible tells us that no one can have peace with God or know the
peace of God without first having believed the gospel message. Jesus is
always the author and giver of inner peace, which cannot be experienced
apart from a relationship with Him. Sin, which separates us from God, and
guilt are the plague of every human heart. So sin must be dealt with and
guilt must be removed before we can experience the joys of being forgiven
or the comforts of knowing we are accepted by God. This can happen only
when we recognize our helpless condition and acknowledge our need for
Christ's forgiveness. Then we must put our faith in the payment for our sin,
which is the precious blood of God's own Son, Jesus Christ.

5. Read Colossians 1:20. By what means do we have peace with God?

When people attempt to earn their own salvation or come to God
through any other means than the blood of Christ, they meet with utter
rejection. They remain enemies of God, lost and in danger of remaining
separated from Him forever. The penalty for our sin cannot be abolished
unless we come to Christ and receive salvation and forgiveness through
faith alone, apart from works.

God does not give peace of mind to *anyone* who rejects the gospel
message. Isaiah 57:21 says that the unsaved have no peace. Verse 20 com-
pares those who reject the Lord to a troubled sea that perpetually churns
up mire and dirt. In stark contrast, Isaiah 32:18 describes believers as
dwelling in a place of peace, in secure dwellings, and quiet resting places.
Fear and inner turmoil always characterize those who do not know Christ
and are not forgiven (Revelation 21:8), but they should never characterize
someone who is in a right relationship to God.

6. According to Romans 5:1, what precedes peace with God?

7. Read Romans 3:10–18. What do these verses reveal about

unregenerate humanity?

8. Read Ephesians 2:14 and 15. What does Christ break down when
   we are saved through faith?

Shalom

The word "Shalom" is translated in our English Bible over 170 times
as "peace." It was used by the Jewish people as a greeting and was meant to
convey a wish for blessing or well-being. In New Testament times, our Lord
Himself used "peace" as a salutation when He greeted His disciples and fol-
lowers. It was also the usual greeting that Paul and other New Testament
writers used in the opening of their letters to fellow Christians. New Testament Christians greeted one another with references to the peace of God
because it is so closely tied to believers' relationship with Christ and is their
unique privilege.

9. Read Luke 10:5. What greeting did the Lord Jesus instruct His disciples to give when they entered a home?

10. What greeting did Jesus speak when He appeared to the disciples
    after the Resurrection, as recorded in Luke 24:36?

11. After the writers of Romans, 2 Peter, 2 John, Jude, and Revelation
    identified the recipients of their letters, what salutation (or greet-
    ing) did they use? (See Romans 1:7, 2 Peter 1:2, 2 John 1:3, Jude
    1:2, and Revelation 1:4.)

Peace of God

12. Peace with God is conditional upon salvation and upon a believer's
    relationship with Christ in obedience and faith. Read the following
    verses of Scripture, noting what condition produces peace in a be-
    liever's heart.

Passage	Condition to Be Fulfilled
Psalm 119:165	
Isaiah 26:3	
Isaiah 32:17	
Isaiah 48:18	
Romans 15:13	
2 Corinthians 13:11	
2 Peter 1:2	

Peace is the absence of fear or turmoil within a believer's heart. It should be the normal state of mind of all who know Christ as their Savior. And it can be, as long as we remember the promises of God and rely upon them. Jesus lived dependent upon the Father, in constant fellowship with the Father, and in absolute confidence of the Father's love and goodwill. Everything He did or said reflected His reliance upon the truths contained in the Word of God. As a result, He exemplified what it is to live in perfect peace. As we study the Gospels, we get little glimpses of the freedom from fear, as well as the joy and contentment, that characterized Christ's heart. This is what the Lord wants for every child of God and what He meant when He said, "Peace I leave with you, my peace I give unto you" (John 14:27). The peace Christ gives is not the peace the world talks about, but is a peace that goes far beyond human understanding and dispels every fear.

13. Read Mark 4:37–41.

(a) Why were the disciples afraid?

(b) Why was Christ able to sleep peacefully?

(c) What do you think Christ wanted His disciples to believe about Him?

(d) What do you believe Christ wants us to learn from this story?

14. The Bible teaches that fear produces torment and that it is not the Father's will for His children. What is the antidote to fear, according to 1 John 4:17 and 18?

15. Read Galatians 5:16 and 17 and 5:22 and 23. Peace is listed as the fruit of God's Spirit. How is this fruit produced in a believer's life?

Neither peace nor joy comes by our efforts to work it up. Peace cannot be found unless it is found in Christ. It eludes the pursuit of those who attempt to grasp it on their own terms. They may momentarily think they have found peace, only to discover it dissolves into thin air like a rainbow in the sky. Counterfeit peace and happiness come and go, but real peace and joy permeate the heart even in the storms of life. Peace that is the product of God's Spirit anchors the soul and withstands the tempests and trials of life. Nowhere in the Bible are we told that peace originates in our own righteous acts or goodness. We experience peace by cultivating our faith, not our righteousness, "for to be carnally minded is death; but to be spiritually minded is life and peace" (Romans 8:6).

Paul described the peace of God as an armed guard, standing at the doors of our hearts and minds and refusing entry to any enemy that would threaten the quiet confidence and contentment that rests within. Paul spoke of peace that surpasses all human comprehension and is supernaturally produced by God's Spirit. The believer's access to this wonderful peace is not automatic, but follows specific actions.

16. Read Philippians 4:4–9. Paul told believers to

(a) Always _____ .

(b) Do not be anxious about _____ .

(c) Pray about _____ .

(d) Be _____ when you pray.

(e) Think about things that are _____

_____ .

(f) Practice what you have _____ and

_____ .

CONCLUDING THOUGHTS

People long for peace, but they look for it in the wrong places. The unbeliever can never find it, but the believer has been promised abundant peace. We look for it in the Lord Jesus Christ, Jehovah-Shalom. He is the author and origin of peace. He alone makes it possible for believers to know the quiet sense of calm assurance that everything is just fine. Let the world rage and let the storms of life come—God does not change and is not perturbed one bit. He still calms the raging storm and still turns disasters into opportunities. He can still make beauty out of ashes, heal wounded hearts, and transform broken hearts and lives. He chases away every fear and fills the heart with joy amid the darkest storms of life. One must simply believe and seek *Him*.

EXPRESS THE TRUTH IN SONG

"Sing, O heavens; and be joyful, O earth; and break forth into singing, O mountains: for the Lord hath comforted his people, and will have mercy upon his afflicted" (Isaiah 49:13).

Like a River Glorious

Like a river glorious is God's perfect peace.
Over all victorious in its bright increase;
Perfect yet it floweth fuller every day.
Perfect yet it growth deeper all the way
Stayed upon Jehovah, Hearts are fully blest
Finding as He promised, perfect peace and rest.
                                        —Francis Havergal

Jehovah-Rohi:
The Lord Our Shepherd

"He shall feed his flock like a shepherd: he shall gather the lambs with his arm, and carry them in his bosom, and shall gently lead those that are with young" (Isaiah 40:11).

Having someone who cares—that's the way we usually describe the best thing about a close, loving relationship. Knowing we have someone who will care about us no matter what happens is a tremendous comfort. Yet it's more than just a comfort; close relationships can make the difference between joy and sorrow and even life or death. From the youngest to the oldest, human beings thrive best in nurturing groups, not alone or isolated. God has created us to interact, so we like to stay connected with people, whether it be people in our immediate families or workplaces, or friends who share in our joys and sorrows.

We also like to know that we have people in our lives who are looking out for our best interests—whether they are loving parents, pastors, doctors, a boss, a child, or government officials. Knowing there is someone on the other end of our 9-1-1 call who is able to immediately summon the fire department, police, or ambulance gives us a sense of security. We *like* knowing that knowledgeable people are in charge and know exactly how to help! When we do not see leadership working on our behalf, we tend to become restless, on edge, or distracted. We don't rest well, and we spend a lot of emotional energy making sure our needs are taken care of.

When God chose to compare us with sheep, He did so with good reason. We share many characteristics common to sheep, including the desire to congregate. And when God chose to compare Himself with a good shepherd, He also did so deliberately, because He exemplifies many characteristics of a kind shepherd who manages every detail of His flock well. God wants us to picture a scene that speaks to our human hearts. He created us and loves us. He wants us to know that there is Someone who cares more than anyone on earth cares, and who knows exactly what to do in any circumstance. Like sheep with a good shepherd, He wants us to feel secure, to rest unperturbed by trouble or care, and to know we are dearly loved and meticulously cared for. So He reminds us, "Know ye that the LORD he is God: it is he that hath made us, and not we ourselves; we are his people, and the sheep of his pasture" (Psalm 100:3). Our God and Savior is Jehovah-Rohi, the Lord our Shepherd.

STUDY THE WORD

The Shepherd of His People

God, as Jehovah in the Old Testament and Jesus in the New, is described as the Shepherd of His people. Many familiar paintings depicting Christ as a Shepherd with a lamb in His arms were inspired by Isaiah 40:11, which is a prophecy concerning Christ. While our God is a consuming fire and the lion of Judah, He is also a tender, caring shepherd who invites us to come into His fold.

1. Read Isaiah 40:11.

   (a) What does this Shepherd do that convinces your heart He is kind and caring and will exercise the same tenderness toward you?

   (b) How is Isaiah 40:11 like 1 Corinthians 10:13?

2. What do Hebrews 13:20 and 21 call Jesus?

Both the Old and New Testaments describe believers as God's sheep and as people who bear the nature of sheep. Sheep do not survive in the wild without someone who skillfully manages their care and protection. Sheep will put themselves in mortal danger in a number of ways, including blindly following the lost, to eating and drinking dangerous things. Sheep are prone to become infested with parasites and pests, and are naturally fearful creatures. They have no natural defense and are easy prey to wild animals. Some sheep will pick fights with other sheep, pushing and controlling less dominant members of the flock. Others insist on wandering off into dangerous areas in search of "better" forage. Without a shepherd to intervene on behalf of the sheep, the flock can easily be destroyed from dangers without and within.

    3. Read Isaiah 53:1–6. How does this passage illustrate Christ's attitude toward us and our natural tendency toward Him?

    4. What did Peter describe in 1 Peter 2:25?

Sheep know who their shepherd is and respond to his presence. When they see him walking among them or hear his voice, they instantly become less fretful, and they follow him. A stranger does not have the same effect. Instead of being comforted by the presence of a stranger, sheep will become troubled or agitated by him. They will refuse to cooperate with or be led by someone they do not know or trust.

    5. Summarize John 10:2–5, emphasizing what Jesus was saying about believers and Himself.

    6. Why, according to John 10:11, is Jesus the Good Shepherd?

God's Shepherding Care

God often referred to Israel as His sheep and described Himself as their shepherd. Many passages of Scripture describe the nature and quality of God's shepherding care and give us a glimpse into the way He shepherds all of His people to this day. Just as He provided everything Israel needed to build a strong nation, so God provides everything we need to live happy, blessed lives (2 Peter 1:3). He provided manna in the desert, and He still gives the sweet manna of His Word to strengthen and sustain His people (Matthew 4:4). God protected the people of Israel when their enemies threatened to destroy them. Likewise, He protects us with weapons that are powerful enough to conquer any foe (2 Corinthians 10:3–6). As God led Israel with a pillar of fire, so He leads us by His Spirit (John 16:13).

Our God uses many means to provide, protect, and guide His people, just as He used David to shepherd His people Israel or used heathen nations to discipline them. The Bible tells us that Jehovah-Rohi guides His people by the skillfulness of His hand. He knows exactly what we need at exactly the right time. As Romans 8:28 promises, God is able to orchestrate and manage every event for our good and His glory.

7. Read Psalm 78:13–16 and 52–55. After each reference, write whether the verse describes God's provision, protection, or guidance.

Verse 13 _____

Verse 14 _____

Verses 15, 16 _____

Verse 52 _____

Verse 53 _____

Verse 54 _____

Verse 55 —————————————————————

The Heritage of God's Sheep

Perhaps no other chapter of the Bible is more read or loved than the Twenty-third Psalm, because it speaks to the human heart and provides comfort. It tells of God's continual presence and care on behalf of His sheep. It calms our fears with gentle words of reassurance. It is often read in times of difficulty or uncertainty. While believers and unbelievers alike have attempted to find comfort in its promises, it was not written by or for unbelievers. Instead, it came from the heart of a believer—one who knew the Great Shepherd personally and had been blessed to experience His marvelous care. Unbelievers have not come under the management of the Good Shepherd, so they cannot make the claims that believing Christians can.

David began the Twenty-third Psalm by exclaiming that Jehovah was *his* Shepherd. David spoke from the perspective of a satisfied sheep who is thrilled to belong to Jehovah and come under His care. David made this claim on the basis that he lacked absolutely nothing, for his Shepherd had carefully provided for him, right down to the last detail. So David wrote, "The LORD is my shepherd; I shall not want." In Psalm 34:9 he said, "There is no want to them that fear him." God's sheep lack nothing, for God is ready and willing to meet every need and to provide, protect, and guide His sheep. David also wrote, "For the LORD God is a sun and shield: the LORD will give grace and glory: no good thing will he withhold from them that walk uprightly" (Psalm 84:11). God's sheep are able to rest content, for God is able to supply every need according to His riches in glory. This is the precious heritage of *all* God's children, the sheep of His pasture.

8. (a) What statement in Psalm 23 testifies that believers will not lack rest or nourishment?

(b) Look up Psalms 4:8 and 145:16. According to them, what does God provide? How do you know?
Psalm 4:8

Psalm 145:16

9. (a) What statement in Psalm 23 indicates that believers will not lack refreshment?

    (b) What phrases in the following verses say that God provides refreshment?
    Isaiah 49:10 (addressed to Israel)

    John 6:35 (addressed to the people who were "seeking for Jesus," verse 24)

10. (a) What statement in Psalm 23 suggests that believers will not lack restoration or forgiveness?

    (b) What phrases in the following verses tell us that God provides restoration, or forgiveness?
    Psalm 86:5

    Psalm 56:13

11. (a) What statement in Psalm 23 demonstrates that believers will not lack guidance?

    (b) What statements imply that God provides believers with guidance?
    Psalm 32:8

    Psalm 48:14

12. (a) What statement in the Twenty-third Psalm indicates that believers will not lack God's presence and protection?

(b) What statements in the following verses tell believers that God will protect and be with them?
Matthew 28:20

Hebrews 13:5

13. (a) What statement in Psalm 23 suggests that God's children will not lack correction or comfort in times of trouble?

(b) What statements in the following verses say that God will both correct and comfort those He loves?
Proverbs 3:12

Jeremiah 31:3

14. (a) What statement in the Twenty-third Psalm implies that believers will not lack God's provision and protection?

(b) What statements in the following verses demonstrate that God provides protection for His sheep?
Psalm 5:11

Psalm 18:17

15. (a) What statement in Psalm 23 indicates that believers will not lack relief in times of suffering?

(b) What words in the following verses indicate that God will provide relief in times of suffering?
Hebrews 4:16

Psalm 147:3

16. (a) What statement in Psalm 23 indicates that believers will not lack God's love and mercy all their lives?

(b) What statements show that God provides love and mercy? Psalm 36:7

James 5:11

17. (a) What statement in Psalm 23 indicates that believers will not lack a future and permanent place with their Lord?

(b) What phrases tell you that God will provide a future home where you, if you are a believer, will live with Him forever? Hebrews 11:16

John 14:2, 3

The Care of God's Sheep

To know Jehovah-Rohi is a blessed privilege and joy, for He is a good shepherd who is full of love and never abandons His sheep or ignores their needs. Hired servants claim to care for the Lord's sheep, but when their own safety or comfort is threatened, these servants run for their lives. Not Christ: He loves the sheep and willingly laid down His life for them.

18. Why does the hireling, or hired servant, flee, according to John 10:13–15?

Mature believers are to look after God's flock and oversee their care. They are to feed God's lambs with God's Word and teach them how to grow in grace, willingly sacrificing themselves for the welfare of God's sheep. Laborers who will genuinely care for poor pitiful sheep are few, and Paul lamented that he had no one, except Timothy, who was willing to minister to the Philippian church and oversee their care and spiritual growth.

    19. What reason did Paul give in Philippians 2:19–21 for this disinterest in the Lord's possession?

    20. How should believers respond to Jehovah-Rohi, who so willingly laid down His life for His sheep and cares for them with amazing love and devotion?

        Psalm 79:13

        Ezekiel 34:6

        Psalm 95:6, 7

        Psalm 89:1

CONCLUDING THOUGHTS

Countless believers have found sweet consolation and joy in knowing Jehovah-Rohi, that great Shepherd of their souls. His benefits are incredible, but best of all, everything that He does for the welfare of His sheep is done with love and tender devotion. Such compassion ought to stir our hearts until we burst with grateful praise and adoration, knowing we are the special objects of His love. May each of us who know Him share our joy with others and plead with lost sheep to enter into the fold through the door, which is Christ, and commit their souls to the safe keeping of our Good Shepherd!

EXPRESS THE TRUTH IN SONG

"I will sing of the mercies of the LORD for ever: with my mouth will I make known thy faithfulness to all generations" (Psalm 89:1).

Surely Goodness and Mercy

A pilgrim was I, and a wandering
In the cold night of sin I did roam,
When Jesus the kind Shepherd found me,
And now I am on my way home.

He restoreth my soul when I'm weary;
He giveth me strength day by day.
He leads me beside the still waters;
He guards me each step of the way.

Chorus

Surely goodness and mercy shall follow me,
All the days, all the days of my life.
Surely goodness and mercy shall follow me,
All the days, all the day of my life.
And I shall dwell in the house of the Lord forever
And I shall feast at the table spread for me.
Surely goodness and mercy shall follow me
All the days, all the days of my life.
                    —John W. Peterson and Alfred B. Smith

Recommended reading: *A Shepherd Looks at the Twenty-Third Psalm* by Phillip Keller.

Jehovah-Sabaoth:
The Lord of Hosts

"As for our redeemer, the LORD of hosts is his name, the Holy One of Israel" (Isaiah 47:4).

A battle is raging, and the stakes are high. This battle does not take place on the battlegrounds of earth but in the hearts of men and women, as the eternal destiny of their souls hangs in the balance. Christians everywhere struggle as they fight the ways of an ungodly world, their own sinful human desires, and the wicked plots of the Devil. It is a universal problem that affects every age group in every generation. This battle is like none other, for we do not fight a visible enemy of flesh and blood. We fight against the unseen things—sin within and without, corruption in high places, malicious intent, and evil in the spiritual realm—that are directed toward thwarting believers' progress (Ephesians 6:12). We fight our fiercest battles within our own minds. It is on this battlefield that all is ultimately won or lost, for as a woman thinks in her heart, so is she (Proverbs 23:7).

The enemy (Satan) has several objectives. He wants to keep people from defecting from his army, and he wants to motivate or inspire soldiers to join him in his hatred and rebellion against the living God. Satan wants to keep the people of God distracted and confused so they will not organize and become a formidable foe. He doesn't want them to conquer sin or keep themselves unspotted from the world. He wants them to befriend the world and indulge their sinful appetites, because he knows the darkness and destruction those choices will bring upon them.

This great enemy of God is a master manipulator, liar, and deceiver. He is malicious and filled with rage toward those who have been redeemed by the blood of Christ. He seeks to instigate contention and discontent among God's people, to make them doubt and fear, fight and complain—for he does not fear a bitter, fearful, discouraged, or defeated foe. He fears only those who dare to put their trust in Christ and raise their swords to fight in the name of Jehovah-Sabaoth, the Lord of Hosts.

STUDY THE WORD

The Lord of Hosts

God did not reveal Himself as Jehovah-Sabaoth until after the Children of Israel were ready to leave the deserts of Sinai and enter the Promised Land. He had revealed Himself as Elohim, the powerful creator God; Jehovah, the personal God who acts on behalf of each individual believer; and I AM, the self-existing, incomprehensible God. But the people of Israel did not yet know Him as Jehovah-Sabaoth, the Lord of Hosts. As Joshua prepared to cross Jordan and take possession of the promises of God, he came face-to-face with the Captain of Heaven's armies, and it changed his life forever. Joshua came to know Jehovah-Sabaoth, the victorious God who would lead the people of Israel into battle and secure the victory for them.

    1. Read Joshua 5:13–15.

        (a) What did Joshua do first when he realized to whom he was talking?

        (b) What was Joshua's attitude when he received a command?

        (c) How did Joshua respond to the Lord?

Like David of old, we win our battles with the evil one when we meet him in the name of the Lord of Hosts, Jehovah-Sabaoth. When Goliath mocked and taunted David, David did not run or cower in fear. He calmly explained by what power he would be victorious.

   2. Read 1 Samuel 17:45–47. What three things did David say the
       people would know after Goliath was conquered?

   3. The details of Israel's battles and experiences have been recorded
       in the Scriptures for a specific reason. According to 1 Corinthians
       10:11, what is that reason?

   4. Read each passage, and then identify the enemy. Is it the ways of
       the world, our own sinful human nature, and/or the works of the
       Devil?
       1 Peter 2:11

       1 John 2:15–17

       1 Peter 5:8

       2 Corinthians 4:4

       Galatians 5:17

   5. In Romans 8:37, how did Paul describe believers?

   6. According to 1 Corinthians 15:57, who does victory come through?

   Our confidence in battle is to be in a Person, not in a strategy and
not in our own abilities. The Lord Jesus Christ is called the captain of our

souls. He is the mighty one in battle, the commander-warrior who ensures victory for His people. Victory depends on our recognizing that the battle is the Lord's, that it is He who fights on our behalf. Our responsibilities are to humble ourselves to follow Him and to step out in faith to face the battle—whether it threatens to overthrow our faith and confidence in Christ or to keep us from experiencing our blessings as God's dear children.

Notice how David prayed in Psalm 35:1–7, asking the Lord to fight his enemy and win the battle on his behalf. Are you facing battles like David's? Have you been mistreated in some way? Responding to this enemy with vengeance and bitterness will give evil a stronghold in your heart, ruining your joy and victory. The way to fight this foe and win by the power of God is to confess and forsake all thoughts of vengeance, anger, or bitterness as sin. Then call upon the Lord of Hosts and rely upon Him to work on your behalf as you handle problems in a righteous way.

7. Compare what you have read in Psalm 35 with Romans 12:19.

(a) What instruction did the Captain of the Host give?

(b) Read Romans 12:20 and 21. In your own words, tell what the Lord tells us to do.

8. Psalm 146:3–5. What is the result when we believers trust the Lord and entrust our battles to Him?

The Christian's Warfare

It was said in ancient times that every Spartan was born a warrior. Certainly, when we are born into the family of God through faith in Christ, we become warriors for our God. This life *is* a battle, and we live in a war zone. To ignore the war and make ourselves comfortable in enemy territory is to place ourselves in a certain path of destruction. Many believers suffer defeat at the hand of the enemy simply because they ignore the battle and imagine that if they don't fight, they won't get hurt. Our self-serving human nature wants to shrink from anything that might require self-sacrifice. It likes to cater instead to its desire for comfort. Pretending that the battlefield is a playground and refusing to acknowledge the danger won't make it a safe place. It will simply guarantee a casualty.

Every believer is to fight the good fight of faith, and all believers have everything they need to win every battle. Believers do not go into battle alone, nor do they fight in their own strength. Believers become victorious as they come to know Jehovah-Sabaoth and submit to His leadership. Believers become battle casualties only when they refuse to fight, or they fight their own way, refusing to use the weapons they have been issued.

The first thing soldiers learn in basic training is to submit to authority. They learn that there is a chain of command and that at the top of the chain is the commander in chief. God wants us to know that He is our commander in chief, the one who has all authority. With it, He has the right to give a command and expect it to be obeyed. The Bible tells us that the myriad chariots of God are at His command and that all the hosts of Heaven respond to His will. He never loses a battle, never orders a retreat, and never gives a bad order; therefore, He can be trusted. David exclaimed in wonder, "O LORD God of hosts, who is a strong LORD like unto thee?" (Psalm 89:8). Christian soldiers who put their trust in Him, submit to Him, and obey Him always win in the end.

The most important principle that Christian soldiers must learn is that they are no match for the enemy and cannot win by focusing their attention on him. Every battle plan and every weapon given to believers rests on this one basic command: each individual believer must submit him- or herself 100 percent to Christ.

The book of James tells us that the way to successfully resist the Devil is to submit to God. Victory over the Devil is ours when we concentrate on obeying Christ, *not* on fighting an elusive enemy.

9. Read James 4:7. What is the result when believers concentrate on

obeying Christ instead of fighting the enemy?

10. Read Colossians 1:16–18. In what areas is Christ to have the pre-eminence?

Old Testament prophets often used the name "Jehovah-Sabaoth" ("Lord of Hosts") when they proclaimed God's commandments to His people. This name emphasized God's authority and right to give a command and to expect obedience. To win our battles, we, too, must submit to God's command.

Secrets of Victory

To be effective soldiers, we must familiarize ourselves with our weapons of warfare and develop skill using them. The only effective weapons available for this war are the ones God has provided for us.

11. (a) Read Ephesians 6:11–17. What is the one piece of battle gear that, above all else, protects believers?

(b) Read 1 John 5:4 and 5. What gives Christians victory over the world?

The commands of our Captain enable us to conquer our enemies. However, obedience requires faith, for we do not readily understand God's ways. We naturally want to follow our own human reasoning, but we cannot fight our personal battles with the weapons of this world and win. Spiritual battles must be fought by spiritual means.

12. Read 2 Corinthians 10:3–6. What battle plan did God give that enables us to take back the enemy's strongholds?

13. The shield of faith spoken of in the New Testament can be built only with the right materials. Read Romans 10:17. What produces faith in a believer's life?

14. Read Matthew 4:10. What "sword" did Jesus use to defeat the temptations of the Devil?

Under the Commander's Protection

At the height of Rome's military power, the world respected and feared the Roman emperor and his army. At his word, a person could be put to death, beaten, or severely punished. Being a citizen of Rome meant that a person had special privileges and could not be put to death without a trial before the Roman court. Nor could he be beaten like a noncitizen. For this reason, the Roman officers mentioned in Acts 22:25–29 became afraid when they learned that they had bound and prepared to scourge a Roman citizen—the apostle Paul.

There is an infinitely greater ruler than the emperor of Rome, and citizens of His country have privileges that far exceed those of a Roman citizen. The Lord of Hosts is in command of the armies of Heaven, and His authority extends over all the earth. It is a fearsome thing when one of His own is mistreated and appeals to Him. The prophet Zechariah warned God's enemies and comforted God's people by saying, "Thus saith the LORD of hosts; . . . he that toucheth you toucheth the apple of his eye" (Zechariah 2:8). When God's children are mistreated or abused, it does not go unnoticed by Jehovah-Sabaoth. God will defend those who are His own.

15. Notice the context in which James used "the Lord of sabaoth" (v. 4) in James 5:1–6. What message was James conveying?

16. Based on what you have learned about the Lord of Hosts, or Lord

of Sabaoth, why should the warning in 1 Thessalonians 4:6–8
cause believers to be careful how we treat one another?

17. Psalm 46 contrasts a frightening world that is out of control with
    a quiet place where believers find peace and strength. The psalm-
    ist used the word "refuge" three times, twice connecting it to the
    name "the Lord of Hosts."
    (a) Find and underline these phrases and the word "refuge" in
        your Bible.
    (b) In your opinion, why did the psalmist use the name "the Lord
        of Hosts" (Jehovah-Sabaoth) in the context of God's being a
        refuge and comfort to His people?

Satan's Strategy with the Lost

The enemy of all mankind wants nothing less than the hearts and
souls of all who remain his prisoners, lost and without Christ. He guards
them and actively works to deceive them into believing that neither he
nor the powers of darkness, nor Christ, exist. The last thing Satan wants
people to know is that they desperately need a Savior. He wants them to
remain oblivious to the battle being waged for their eternal souls. He wants
those who are held captive to believe that there is no way of escape from
the bondage of their sin and that no one would risk his own life to rescue
them. The Devil, who is called a roaring lion seeking whom he may devour,
wants no one to get a glimpse of life "on the outside," free from his tyr-
anny and power.

18. Read Acts 26:17 and 18, 2 Corinthians 4:4, and 2 Timothy 2:26.
    What is Satan's method of keeping people from understanding
    their need for salvation?

One of the cleverest ways Satan keeps unbelievers "in the dark" is to showcase Christians who live carelessly and fall prey to the devastations of sin. These Christians bring a reproach upon, or disapproval of, the cause of Christ and give the Devil fuel for his lies. As the day of Christ's return draws near, let us cast off the works of darkness and put on the armor of light, as Paul exhorted in Romans 13:12, lest we contribute to the misconceptions of the lost.

19. Read 2 Corinthians 2:11. How does Satan get an advantage over believers?

CONCLUDING THOUGHTS

The wiles of the Devil bring the battles of evil to the doorstep of every person's daily life. Christians often shrink in terror, for they hear the sounds of battle, see the devastations of others, and lose their confidence in Christ. This is, perhaps, one of Satan's most effective tools to keep Christians from winning their battles and rejoicing in victories—he simply keeps them afraid and discouraged. He doesn't want believers to understand that victory is always certain when they pick up the sword of the Spirit, the Word of God, and lift the shield of faith, which extinguishes every attack of the Devil. If believers become spiritual casualties because of trials, it is only because they went AWOL in the Lord's army and refused to fight under God's command.

When we focus on problems and difficulties, we become disheartened. Our spirits are revived with hope when we look instead to the Captain of the Host, our God and our Savior. He has already won for us the greatest victory of all, having slain our enemy death. Believers must never forget that we are powerless in battle but that He is the mighty one who enables us to triumph over every trial. The righteous (that's believers) have many afflictions, as Scripture reminds us, but the Lord delivers us out of them all (Psalm 34:19). When we open our eyes of faith, we see what the world cannot see—the angels of the Lord encamping about our dwelling with swords drawn and chariots gleaming (see 2 Kings 6:15), ready to fight and defend at the word of our Commander. We are on the winning side, and we win by the word of truth, by the power of God, and by the armor of righteousness on the right hand and on the left (2 Corinthians 6:7).

David was a warrior who learned the lessons of faith in Jehovah-Sabaoth and celebrated many incredible victories as a result. Knowing God and resting in His leadership and power as commander in chief brought David joy. As he thought back over his life and recalled the Lord's faithfulness and power, David sang and praised the King of Kings and Lord of Lords. In Psalm 24 he asked, "Who is this King of glory?" and then replied to the rhetorical question by exclaiming, "The LORD strong and mighty, the LORD mighty in battle." Then to emphasize his point, he asked once more, "Who is this King of glory?" and then triumphantly replied once again, "The LORD of hosts, he is the King of glory" (Psalm 24:8, 10).

EXPRESS THE TRUTH IN SONG

"O sing unto the LORD a new song; for he hath done marvellous things: his right hand, and his holy arm, hath gotten him the victory" (Psalm 98:1).

Sound the Battle Cry

Sound the battle cry! See the foe is nigh;
Raise the standard high for the Lord;
Gird your armor on, stand firm, everyone;
Rest your cause upon His Holy Word.

O Thou God of all, Hear us when we call,
Help us one and all by thy grace;
When the battle's done, and the victory's won,
May we wear the crown before Thy face.

Chorus

Rouse, then, soldiers, rally round the banner,
Ready, steady, pass the word along;
Onward, forward, shout aloud Hosanna!
Christ is Captain of the mighty throng.
                                        —William F. Sherwin

Jehovah-Tsidkenu:
The Lord Our Righteousness

"This is his name whereby he shall be called, The LORD OUR RIGHTEOUSNESS" (Jeremiah 23:6).

The vilest criminal incarcerated for his crimes has something in common with the most selfless citizen honored for his service. Both are compelled to find satisfaction in some good thing they have done or in some good character trait they possess. Both will find someone worse than themselves, and both will find comfort by judging themselves better than those others. It is inherent in human nature to compare oneself with others to appease guilt and to feel acceptable, righteous, or justified. People are prone to engage in this futile exercise, no matter how good or how bad they may be. While no woman can be good enough to believe she is perfect, each one can judge herself better than someone else and, therefore, can find a perverted sense of comfort in that knowledge.

Attempts to find inner peace by comparing oneself with others always fails, no matter how much "better" one perceives herself to be. No one is good enough to be reconciled to God on the basis of her own merit, and no one—not even a believer—can come boldly to the throne of God on the basis of her flawless obedience or impeccable life. Those who imagine they deserve God's favor discover, as the Pharisees did, that God's mercy is withheld and their prayer is vain.

STUDY THE WORD
1. Read Luke 18:10–14. Why did the publican walk away "justified"?

By comparing ourselves to others, we might be able to temporarily convince ourselves that we are righteous enough to be accepted by God. But we find ourselves falling miserably short of perfection if we compare ourselves to the faultless Son of God—no matter who we are. Neither salvation nor the assurance and joy of salvation can be experienced apart from knowing Jehovah-Tsidkenu. For it is in the meaning of this name that we discover God's solution to our "righteousness" dilemma!

God Our Righteousness

The name "Jehovah-Tsidkenu" is introduced in the book of Jeremiah and means, "Jehovah Our Righteousness." It does not simply mean, "Jehovah is righteous," though of course He is perfectly righteous. The wonder of this name is that "Jehovah-Tsidkenu" means "Jehovah is *our* righteousness." We can never be accepted by God on the basis of our own righteousness, for we can never be righteous *enough* to fellowship with the holy and perfect One. We must have a completely pure and perfect righteousness to approach Jehovah. We must have nothing less than *His* righteousness imputed (attributed or credited) as our own. Those who thoroughly understand and believe this great truth experience tremendous peace that forever ends the emotional roller coaster of spiritual doubt and fear.

2. Read Psalm 89:16. In what did the people rejoice?

In the days of Jeremiah, the Southern Kingdom (Judah) was an ungodly and idolatrous nation, bent on violence and moral and political corruption. Though the Northern Kingdom (Israel) had gone into captivity a hundred years earlier for the same sins, Judah ignored all of God's warnings and was about to suffer the same judgment as Israel. It is at this point that Jeremiah described a coming righteous King who will rule justly in contrast to Israel's and Judah's unrighteous kings. Though they had forsaken their God, God had not forsaken them and was promising a coming King who was to be called Jehovah-Tsidkenu, the Lord Our Righteousness.

3. Read Jeremiah 23:5–8. Who was the prophet Jeremiah talking

about when he referred to a coming King who would be a righteous descendant of David?

4. Read Jeremiah 33:14–16. (In verse 16, "Lord" in capital letters represents the name "Jehovah.") Who is Jehovah Our Righteousness?

5. Who is referred to as God in Hebrews 1:8 and 9?

The book of Romans begins by declaring that the heathen are not righteous and, in chapter 2, that Israel is not righteous. In chapter 3, Paul gave yet more evidence of mankind's unrighteous character.

6. Read Romans 3:10–12 and 23. Describe the moral condition of humanity.

7. Who is perfectly righteous, according to Psalm 145:17?

Suppose that the most godly people in the world came together for a "Righteous Olympics," with the winner receiving the title "Most Righteous Living Person." Contestants would be judged on their reputations, good deeds, devotion to God, level of self-sacrifice, acts of love and kindness, and purity of motives. If such a contest existed, even the most righteous person of all time could not come even close to being righteous enough to stand in God's presence, let alone to live in Heaven with Him.

8. Read Isaiah 64:6 and 7. How does God view us and our human righteousness?

Peace with God

We were made to fellowship with God and enjoy His presence, but
our sinful human nature makes fellowship with the perfect and holy One
impossible. Until our sin is confessed and forgiven, an estrangement exists
between us and our Creator. It eats at our consciences and leaves an emotional void in our hearts. Try as we might to commend ourselves to God on
the basis of our own goodness, we constantly fail to experience the joy or
comforts that accompany reconciliation with God. Some people give up in
despair and yield to the pull of their human depravity; others strive to be
acceptable enough to win God's favor, and they hope they are good enough.
Nevertheless, no one clothed in her own righteousness finds forgiveness or
peace with God. Peace cannot be ours until we find it on God's terms.

 9. Read Romans 5:1. By what means do we have peace with God?

"Good" behavior or righteous works are as inadequate to cover failure
and sin as Adam's and Eve's fig leaves were to cover the couple's nakedness.
To walk with God and live in His presence requires perfect obedience and
flawless devotion, which are impossible for Adam's fallen race. Without the
garment of God's perfection covering us completely, we cannot approach
God, let alone enjoy His love and favor. No matter how hard we might try
or how devoted we might be to living more righteously than others, we
cannot be reconciled with God on the basis of our own efforts. We need a
Savior who can take away the reproach of our sin and can live a perfect
and obedient life in our place.

The word "justified" means "to be pronounced righteous." To be justified is not the same thing as being pardoned. A pardon involves excusing
an offense without exacting a penalty. God's justice requires that the penalty for our sins be paid in full. Our sins are not excused—the Lord Jesus
Christ suffered and died to pay for each one.

 10. Read Galatians 2:16, remembering that God has said in Romans
     3:10 that there is "none righteous." A person can never be pro-
     nounced righteous, or perfect, by God by keeping His law. How,

then, can a person be pronounced perfect, or righteous?

11. In Isaiah 53:5 and 6, the prophet Isaiah told of Christ's work on earth. For what purpose did Christ suffer and die?

12. Jesus satisfied the justice of God by paying for all our sin at Calvary.
   (a) According to 2 Corinthians 5:18–21, what does God give to those who believe and put their trust in the finished work of Christ rather than in their own righteousness?

   (b) Who is able to reconcile us to God?

Righteousness by Faith

Charles H. Spurgeon preached a sermon titled "Jehovah Tsidkenu: The Lord Our Righteousness" in which he said: "When we believe in Christ, by faith we receive our justification. As the merit of his blood takes away our sin, so the merit of his obedience is imputed to us for righteousness. We are considered, as soon as we believe, as though the works of Christ were our works. . . . God considers us as though we were Christ—looks upon us as though his life had been our life—and accepts, blesses, and rewards us as though all that he did had been done by us, his believing people."

Justification is a change in God's records whereby our sins are blotted out and the righteousness of Jesus Christ is credited to us. Those who are "righteous" in God's sight are those who have repented of their own unrighteousness and have trusted instead in the finished work of Christ on their behalf.

13. Read Psalm 5:12. Who does God bless with favor?

14. In Romans 10:1–4, Paul addressed religious, disciplined people who believed in God and worshiped Him meticulously yet were not saved. According to verse 3, why weren't these people saved?

15. Compare Ephesians 2:8 and 9 with Romans 10:8–13. We are given the righteousness of Christ as a gift from God when we do what two things?

Accepted in the Beloved

To be clothed in the righteousness of Christ, not our own righteousness, makes us thoroughly and eternally "accepted in the beloved" (Ephesians 1:6). None of our good works add anything to the righteousness of Christ, and not one of our sins and failures takes anything from His righteousness. Nothing we can do will make Him accept or love us more than He already does, and nothing we do will make Him love or accept us less. We who have trusted Christ and renounced all reliance upon anything else stand redeemed, forgiven, and wholly justified before God on His merits alone and by His righteousness alone. Nothing can be laid to our charge because we are God's elect, whom God Himself has forgiven and justified (Romans 8:33). Though our own consciences acknowledge our constant failures and sins, there is no condemnation to us who have trusted Christ. Our God disciplines us as a loving father disciplines children who are beloved, yet He never rejects or disowns us.

16. It is not to our own praise or by our own worthiness that we are accepted by Christ. According to Ephesians 1:6 and 7, to what do we give praise for our acceptance?

We are not saved or made righteous by our good works, but were saved by God's grace to *do* good works and to live by faith in God's Word

(Ephesians 2:10). Though everything done in our bodies will be judged and rewarded in eternity, our righteousness and salvation depend on none of them.

    17. The righteousness we seek is the same righteousness that the apostle Paul spoke of in Philippians 3:8 and 9.

        (a) Describe the righteousness Paul rejected.

        (b) Describe the righteousness he valued.

CONCLUDING THOUGHTS

    The same God who gave the law—which is perfect, just, and good—kept the law perfectly. Jehovah, as the promised Messiah, came to earth as a man and obeyed the law without a single fault. He loved and worshiped God without the slightest lapse in His devotion. He loved His neighbors, both enemies and friends alike (as the Scriptures command), and He willingly suffered abuse at their hands without so much as a hateful thought toward any. He humbled Himself as none other has ever done. He took upon Himself the form of a servant though He was in fact the Almighty Creator. He was perfectly obedient, even unto death on the cross, suffering unspeakable agony for sins He did not commit, all for the love of helpless and unworthy sinners. This is the righteousness that God requires, and this is the righteousness God gives to us when we come to Him by faith.

    The righteousness of Christ is flawless and complete. He lived the life none of us could live, and He is what none of us can ever be on our own—perfectly righteous. He invites us to look to Him to find our joy in His perfect righteousness, which we can receive as our very own. He invites us to look away from our own human frailties, failures, and defeats. This perfect righteousness of Christ is what God sees when He looks upon those who have been redeemed by the blood of Christ, for Christ is truly "the Lord Our Righteousness." "Jehovah-Tsidkenu" is perhaps the most comforting and precious name a believer can know. What joy is ours when we speak this sacred name with understanding and gratitude for what He has done!

Jehovah Tsidkenu, the Lord Our Righteousness

I once was a stranger to grace and to God,
I knew not my danger, and felt not my load;
Though friends spoke in rapture of Christ on the tree,
Jehovah Tsidkenu was nothing to me.

I oft read with pleasure, to soothe or engage,
Isaiah's wild measure and John's simple page;
But e'en when they pictured the blood-sprinkled tree,
Jehovah Tsidkenu seemed nothing to me.

Like tears from the daughters of Zion that roll,
I wept when the waters went over His soul;
Yet thought not that my sins had nailed to the tree
Jehovah Tsidkenu—'twas nothing to me.

When free grace awoke me, by light from on high,
Then legal fears shook me, I trembled to die;
No refuge, no safety in self could I see—
Jehovah Tsidkenu my Saviour must be.

My terrors all vanished before the sweet name;
My guilty fears banished, with boldness I came
To drink at the fountain, life-giving and free—
Jehovah Tsidkenu is all things to me.

Jehovah Tsidkenu! my treasure and boast,
Jehovah Tsidkenu! I ne'er can be lost;
In Thee I shall conquer by flood and by field—
My cable, my anchor, my breastplate and shield!

Even treading the valley, the shadow of death,
This watchword shall rally my faltering breath;
For while from life's fever my God sets me free,
Jehovah Tsidkenu my death-song shall be.

—Robert Murray McCheyne

Note: *This song can be sung to the tune of "My Jesus I Love Thee" (GORDON).*

EXPRESS THE TRUTH IN SONG

"They shall abundantly utter the memory of thy great goodness, and shall sing of thy righteousness" (Psalm 145:7).

Seek Ye First

Seek ye first the kingdom of God
And His righteousness;
And all these things shall be added unto you.
Al-le-lu, Alleluia.

Ask and it shall be given unto you.
Seek and ye shall find.
Knock and the door shall be opened unto you.
Al-le-lu, Alleluia.

Man shall not live by bread alone,
But by every word;
That proceeds from the mouth of God.
Al-le-lu, Alleluia.

—**Karen Lafferty**

Adonai: Our Lord and Our God

"I will praise thee, O Lord my God, with all my heart: and I will glorify thy name for evermore" (Psalm 86:12).

How do you address God in prayer or refer to Him in conversation? Do you prefer to use words such as "Father," "God," or "Jesus"? Are you among those who use the title "Lord" most often?

In all probability, you are like most people and haven't thought a whole lot about the way you address God—you simply incorporate familiar, comfortable words into your prayers and conversations. You might wonder why it matters or why someone might choose one name over another. Actually, the names and titles we use *do* matter; for God uses them with precise purpose, and He takes note of the way we use them, as well. Although God's names and titles reveal a great deal about who God is— the names we use for Him reveal a great deal about who we *believe* God is. There are many good reasons to study and use the names of God appropriately. But important to God is our desire to simply know and please Him in the way we express who He is to us personally.

STUDY THE WORD

1. Read Mark 10:17 and 18.

(a) What did the rich young ruler call Jesus?

(b) What did this title reveal about the man's beliefs?

(c) Why did it matter to Jesus?

2. Read John 20:26–31.
   (a) How did Thomas address Jesus?

   (b) Why was this significant?

3. Read Luke 6:46 and 47.
   (a) What did Jesus say the people called Him?

   (b) Why do you believe Jesus called it to their attention?

Adonai, Elohim, and Jehovah

Beginning in lesson 1 we learned that three primary names of God are used in the Old Testament, each having a specific meaning and purpose. Can you remember how each one is represented in most English Bibles?

4. Complete the following sentences.
   (a) Elohim is translated "_____."

   (b) Yahweh/Jehovah is translated as either "_____" or "_____."

   (c) Adonai is translated "_____."

As we've seen in past chapters, "Elohim" represents God the powerful, the God who can. "Yahweh" or "Jehovah" represents God the personal, the God who acts personally for me and you. The third name, "Adonai," represents God as Authority, the God whom believers obey. Although "Adonai" (translated into English as "Lord") often expresses familiarity or affection, its truest meaning is often misunderstood. "Adonai" denotes one who is master, or one having authority, and is applied in the Old Testament Scriptures to both God and man. When used of God, the first letter is capitalized, and the word expresses sovereign dominion and possession. When used of humans, the entire word is printed in lowercase and expresses delegated authority or ownership of some kind.

In *The Bible Exposition Commentary,* Warren Wiersbe noted, "We can see the correspondence between the Old Testament word 'Adonai' and the New Testament word *Kurios*, in Jesus' quotation of Psalm 110:1."[1]

Psalm 110:1 says, "The LORD said unto my Lord ["Adonai"], Sit thou at my right hand, until I make thine enemies thy footstool." Jesus quoted it in Matthew 22:44, saying, "The LORD said unto my Lord [Greek *kurios*], Sit thou on my right hand, till I make thine enemies thy footstool." Basically, Jesus was asking, If Messiah is David's Son, how can Messiah be David's Lord? The answer is that "as God, Messiah is David's Lord; as man, He is David's Son. He is both 'the root and the offspring of David' (Revelation 22:16). Psalm 110:1 teaches the deity and the humanity of Messiah. He is David's Lord, and He is David's Son." [2]

Lord and Master

To address God the Father or Jesus as "Lord" implies that He is our "Master" to whom we willingly submit and whom we serve. We should never use that name if we are not sincere in our desire to honor His lordship and wholly submit ourselves to Him. He wants to be more than simply "the" Lord: Christ wants to hear the words "our Lord" and "my Lord" as an expression of our personal trust and submission to His authority. It is one thing to believe that Christ is God, but quite another to confess Him to be *our* God and *our* personal Lord.

Three days after Jesus was crucified, Mary Magdalene visited the sepulcher where His body had been laid. Upon seeing the stone rolled away and the body gone, she began to weep. A man she supposed was the gardener appeared and asked why she wept. Not realizing who He was, she continued talking. Then Jesus merely spoke her name, and immediately she

recognized Him. Mary's first words to the risen Christ revealed the attitude
of her heart.

    5. Read John 20:14–16.

      (a) What did Mary call Jesus?

      (b) What do you believe Mary's response expressed?

God's Authority

A lord has authority, legal power, or a right to command or to act. A
landlord oversees and controls his property. Parents exercise authority over
their children, a police officer over a criminal, and a teacher over her classroom. All human authority is delegated, temporary, limited, imperfect, and
subject to a higher authority, which is God. In contrast, God's authority is
absolute, unlimited, unquestioned, perfect, just, and righteous. Only God is
worthy of our absolute, unquestioning trust and obedience.

    6. Read Matthew 28:18. How much authority over Heaven and earth
      has Jesus been given?

    7. In Matthew 23:8–12, what instruction does Christ give to believers
      with regard to exalting any authority above God?

God wants us to submit ourselves to His authority as an act of our
wills. Willing submission expresses our belief that He is worthy to be worshiped and obeyed. Those who refuse to submit their wills to Christ do not
believe He is good and gracious or worthy of trust, while those who willingly submit to Him do so because they believe He is what He has said He
is. Submission, then, is the response of faith, as well as devotion.

    8. Read Psalm 34:8. What happens to a person who experiences/rec-
      ognizes that God is good?

Jesus Is Lord

Whether someone acknowledges Jesus as *her* Lord, or Lord at all, does not change the fact that *He is Lord* of all! We do not "make Him Lord" of our lives—He *is* Lord over *every* life, for He created and owns all life. We merely acknowledge His lordship and submit ourselves to Him, or we do not. As Lord, Jesus has the right to command everything and everyone and to expect obedience. The disciples marveled that even the wind and sea obeyed Him. Though God has granted people the choice to obey or disobey Him, one day—either in this life, or in the life to come—every knee shall bow to Him. Every person will acknowledge Christ's authority and confess that He is God and Lord of all.

9. (a) With what character qualities did God describe Himself in Isaiah 45:21–24?

(b) Why should every person submit to God?

10. According to 1 Timothy 6:14–16, what will our Lord Jesus Christ one day reveal Himself to be, when He appears in all His glory and power?

The very act of responding to the gospel message involves recognition of and submission to God's absolute authority. When we "believe on the Lord Jesus Christ," we are acknowledging His position of authority. Believers are referred to as those who have obeyed the gospel, while unbelievers are referred to as those who "know not God" and who "obey not the gospel of our Lord Jesus Christ" (2 Thessalonians 1:8).

11. According to Acts 17:30, what does God—because He has absolute authority to do so—command all people everywhere to do?

Servant of the Lord

Servants submit to authority. They promote the interests of others and seek to be of service, not for their own benefit, but for the benefit of those they serve. Addressing Christ as "Lord" implies that we are willing to put aside our own interests in order to embrace Christ's desires as our own. To refer to Him as "my Lord" or "our Lord" acknowledges our position as servants and Christ's position as sovereign king of our lives. When it springs from a sincere heart of devotion, it is a precious and personal expression of our deep respect and love for our Savior and God. Such devotion and submission *always* manifest themselves outwardly in service to Him.

Jesus humbled Himself to serve others, providing a living example of the servant-heart that Christians are to emulate. We read in Philippians 2:7 that Christ took upon Himself the form of a servant and sacrificially gave Himself to meet the legitimate needs of others. We are to serve others with this same sacrificial spirit as an expression of our love for them and for the Lord.

12. Read John 13:12–17. What is the result of knowing and following Christ's example of serving others?

13. How did the believers mentioned in Hebrews 6:10 serve Christ and show love toward His name?

14. Read Exodus 4:10.
    (a) What words did Moses use to address God?

    (b) How did Moses refer to himself in relationship to God?

15. Which believers are mentioned as the Lord's servants in the following verses?
    Exodus 4:10–13

Psalm 18:1

Romans 1:1

Romans 16:1

James 1:1

2 Peter 1:1

Jude 1:1

CONCLUDING THOUGHTS

Knowing the full implications of the name "Adonai" ought to cause us to examine the way we use the word "Lord." It should never become a flippant name, spoken out of habit or mere formality. Rather, it should be a name spoken with the utmost reverence and devotion. God knows the thoughts and intents of our hearts. He knows what we mean when we call Him "Lord," just as He knew the hearts of those who called Him "Lord" while He walked upon the earth. Some addressed Him as "Lord" and did not mean what they said, while others called Him "Lord" with hearts full of sincerity and faith. May we be so filled with love and gratitude for our God that our lips cannot suppress the words, "my Lord and my God." And may we mean it in the truest sense of the word to the delight of Jesus, our gracious Lord and Savior.

EXPRESS THE TRUTH IN SONG

"Serve the LORD with gladness: come before his presence with singing" (Psalm 100:2).

I Sing a New Song

I sing a new song
Since Jesus came.
Serve a new master,
Wear a new name.
Walk a new road,
Have a new goal.
Know a new peace,
Down deep in my soul.

—Beatrice Bush Bixler

Notes:

1. Warren W. Wiersbe, *The Bible Exposition Commentary* (Wheaton, Ill.: Victor Books, 1989).

2. Ibid.

LEADER'S GUIDE

SUGGESTIONS FOR LEADERS

The Bible is a living and powerful book! It is God speaking to us today. Every opportunity to learn from it is a precious privilege. As you use this study guide, be flexible. It is simply a tool to aid in the understanding of God's Word. Adapt it to suit your unique group of women and their needs. Use the questions as you see fit; the answers are provided to clarify my intent and stimulate your thoughts. You may have an entirely different insight as the Holy Spirit illumines your heart and mind.

The effectiveness of a group Bible study usually depends on two things: the leader herself and the ladies' commitment to prepare beforehand and to interact during the study. You cannot totally control the second factor, but you have total control over the first one. These brief suggestions will help you be an effective Bible study leader.

You will want to prepare each lesson a week in advance. During the week, read supplemental material and look for illustrations in the everyday events of your life as well as in the lives of others.

Encourage the ladies in the Bible study to complete each lesson before the meeting itself. This preparation will make the discussion more interesting. You can suggest that ladies answer two or three questions a day as part of their daily Bible reading time rather than trying to do the entire lesson at one sitting.

You may also want to encourage the ladies to memorize the key verse for each lesson. (This is the verse that is printed in italics at the start of each lesson.) If possible, print the verses on 3" x 5" cards to distribute each week. If you cannot do this, suggest that the ladies make their own cards and keep them in a prominent place throughout the week.

The physical setting in which you meet will have some bearing on the study itself. An informal circle of chairs, chairs around a table, someone's living room or family room—these types of settings encourage people to relax and participate. In addition to an informal setting, create an atmosphere in which ladies feel free to participate and be themselves.

You can plan your own format or adapt this one to meet your needs.

1½-hour Bible Study

10:00—10:30	Bible study
	Leader guides discussion of half the questions in the day's lesson.
10:30—10:45	Coffee and fellowship
10:45—11:15	Bible study
	Leader continues discussion of the questions in the day's lesson.
11:15—11:30	Prayer time

ANSWERS FOR LEADER'S USE

Answers are provided for Bible study questions. Answers for personal questions are not usually provided. Information inside parentheses ( ) is additional instruction for the group leader.

Lesson 1

1. "Eve" means "mother of all living."

2. (a) Rehoboth. (b) After striving with herdsmen of Gerar over two other wells, Isaac moved to a third, and the strife ended. Isaac named it Rehoboth, meaning "there is room," to reflect what had happened.

3. On two occasions Jacob met with God there. The first time, God spoke to Jacob in a dream. He saw angels moving up and down a ladder that ascended into the sky. Jacob then chose to follow God. Since God had spoken to him there, and since Jacob connected God's speaking and His presence with His house, he named the place "house of God," or Bethel.

4. (a) " Mara" means "bitter." Naomi was grieved because of the loss of her husband and two sons. (b) God knew the purpose and future He had for Naomi. Because He forgives and restores, Naomi would once again know joy and be a delight.

5. *Peleg (division)*—The earth was divided at the time of his birth. *Isaac (laughter)*—His mother and father laughed when they were told of his conception. No doubt they laughed with joy at his birth. *(Esau (red)*— His complexion was ruddy at birth. *Jacob (supplanter)*—Born a twin, he was delivered from the womb with his hand clutching his brother's heel.

6. Solomon would be a man of peace, unlike his father, David, who was a man of war. During Solomon's reign, Israel would enjoy peace and quietness.

7. Jesus came to die to save people from their sin.

8. *Jezreel (God sows)*—God would avenge the death of Jezreel. *Loruhamah (no mercy)*—God would no longer show mercy to Israel (i.e., the Northern Kingdom). *Loammi (not my people)*—God no longer considered Israel to be His people. (This does not mean He has voided

or canceled His covenants with the nation of Israel. It refers only to the Northern Kingdom.)

9. "Abram" means "father," but "Abraham" means "father of many nations," which is what God told Abraham he would become.

10. (a) The prince of the eunuchs changed "Daniel" to "Belteshazzar," "Hananiah" to "Shadrach," "Mishael to "Meschach," and "Azariah" to "Abednego." (b) Pharaoh changed Joseph's name to Zaphnath-Paaneah.

11. *Psalm 147:5 ("Lord")*—Adonai; *Genesis 1:1 ("God")*—Elohim; *Exodus 6:6 ("Lord")*—Jehovah.

12. (a) Israel (a prince of God)—Israel would be God's people. (b) Samuel (asked of God)—Samuel's mother asked God for a child.

13. "Emmanuel" means "God with us," so it reveals that Christ (Emmanuel) is God.

14. To believe in the name of the Son of God means to put our trust in all that Christ is and all He did, relying upon Him for our salvation.

15. (a) No. (b) There is no other who is able to save us from our sin.

16. Possible answer: The more we know about a person's character and trustworthiness (in this case God's), the more we are able to confidently put our joyful trust in that person.

Lesson 2

1. (a) "Memorial" means "serving to preserve remembrance, commemorative." So a memorial is something that keeps remembrance alive. (b) God wants all future generations to know who He is and the significance of this name.

2. All life originates in God.

3. (a) Christ did not begin in Bethlehem. (b) Christ was present with the Father in creation.

4. (a) He is God, the promised Messiah. (b) Other religious leaders (e.g., Muhammad, Buddha) did not claim to be God.

5. He does not change.

6. God is not only loving in all His ways, but He is the very essence and origin of real love.

7. God is holy, gracious, righteous, and merciful.

8. *Genesis 15:1*—That He is Israel's shield and exceedingly great reward. *Genesis 15:7*—That He is the Lord. *Genesis 17:1*—That He is the Almighty God. *Exodus 6:7*—That He is the Lord God of Israel. *Exodus 22:27*—That He is gracious ("compassionate" in the NIV). *Isaiah 43:3*—That He is God, the Holy One of Israel, and their Savior. *Jeremiah 3:12*—That He is merciful.

9. (a) I AM. (b) Jehovah ("LORD"). (c) Elohim ("GOD").

10. (a) When Jesus called Himself "I AM," He was referring to the God of the exodus. (b) He was saying that He is the God revealed in Exodus. (c) Jesus is God.

11. It establishes God's authority and His right to command.

12. *Leviticus 20:8*—Sanctified them. *Leviticus 22:32*—Made them holy. *Isaiah 43:25*—Forgave their sin. *Isaiah 44:24*—Created everything. *Isaiah 48:17*—Taught and led them. *Isaiah 51:12*—Comforts them. *Jeremiah 9:24*—Loved them and established justice and righteousness on earth.

13. We should take pleasure in the fact that we can understand and know the Lord and know that He exercises loving-kindness, judgment, and righteousness in the earth.

14. God wants us to know that He alone is worthy of glory and worship. Mankind, on the other hand, is not to be worshiped and is not to take credit for God's work.

15. Knowing more about God's character enables us to be confident He will comfort and guide us, and will meet our every need in any trial.

Lesson 3

1. Jeremiah's confidence lay in the truth that since God could create the world, He can do anything, including help Jeremiah (and us) deal with any problem.

2. (a) "Faithful Creator." (b) Possible answer: Christians can trust God to create something beautiful out of our trials.

3. They did not know the Scriptures or God's power.

4. (a) "How excellent is thy name in all the earth!" (b) It caused him to realize that mankind is insignificantly small and weak in comparison to God's greatness and power.

5. (a) By His word. (b) With His word. (c) By speaking the word.

6. By faith.

7. Jehovah, Elohim, Elohim, elohim.

8. The heavens and the earth (i.e., creation).

9. (a) That He is powerful and has authority. (b) Failure: did not give God glory for what He had done; consequence: without excuse. Failure: were not thankful to God; consequence: foolish hearts darkened. Failure: professed themselves to be wise; consequence: became fools. (c) They worship mankind and creation rather than the God who created it all.

10. That He created heaven and earth. God created the earth to be inhabited. There is no other God or creator. God does not keep these things a secret. God rewards those who seek Him. God always righteously speaks what is right. God alone is God, and He alone has the ability to save from sin. The gods created by men have no power. Ultimately, every person will acknowledge who God is.

11. Jesus.

12. That He will finish what He has begun in our lives.

13. A potter.

14. Both are accomplished by God's power.

15. Seeing the wonder, beauty, intricate care, and design—as well as God's awesome power—assures us that we are not too hard for God! He can work in our lives. We can trust Him to complete what He began.

16. Not one star fails. God never tires. God is all-powerful. He gives power to the faint, strength to the weak, and renewed strength to those who wait on Him.

17. Personal answers.

Lesson 4

1. *Proverbs 21:1*—God has power to change the heart of a king. *2 Corinthians 9:8*—God has power and grace to enable us to do His will.

2 Peter 2:9—God has power to deliver us from trials and temptation.

2. People who know God's name (know His character) will trust Him.

3. He committed Himself to God, knowing that God would judge righteously.

4. *Romans 12:18–21*—God will exercise vengeance/judgment. *Exodus 22:22, 23; Deuteronomy 10:17, 18*—God will hear the cry of the fatherless and widows and will exercise judgment against those who wrong them. *1 Thessalonians 4:6*—God will avenge Christians who are wronged by other Christians.

5. That God is the most high over all the earth.

6. All power, greatness, glory, victory, majesty is God's. All of creation belongs to God. God is the head/authority of all His creation. God enables people to have riches and honor. God rules over all. God has the power to make a person great or give strength. All that people give to God came from God.

7. (a) They obey and seek God. (b) They rebelled against His Word, His authority. (c) They acknowledge God's power and cry out to Him for deliverance. (d) Personal answers.

8. Every knee will bow, and every tongue will confess that Jesus Christ is Lord.

9. Honor and obey God, for He has the right to govern our lives.

10. (a) Five. (b) To be exalted like God. (c) Pride.

11. They did not want to obey Him or submit themselves to Him. Other possible answers: They were unthankful for what God had done for them; they did not recognize all God had done for them; they were proud and rebellious against God; they did not know God's character; they were unbelieving.

12. (a) Humility. (b) Pride.

13. God gave the king of Babylon the ability to do great things.

14. God gives us the ability to do great things.

15. Servants of the most high God.

16. God wanted him to know that "the most High" rules in the

kingdom of men, and gives it to whom He chooses.

17. Because God receives all the glory for what is accomplished.

18. That very hour, he became insane and was isolated.

19. He acknowledged that God's dominion is everlasting and that God ("the most High") reigns forever.

20. (a) His pride. (b) His pride and unwillingness to submit to God's authority even though he knew what had happened to Nebuchadnezzar.

21. Personal responses.

Lesson 5

1. (a) Where have you come from, and where will you go? (b) Return home and submit to Sarah. (c) That He would multiply her descendants. (d) That she would have a son, and he would be named Ishmael. (e) Because God had heard her cry and had come to her rescue.

2. (a) "Thou God seest me." (b) "Well of the Living One seeing me." (c) It conveys that God takes note of all that happens on earth, down to the minutest details. He is full of compassion when people experience heartache, and He is always present to guide and comfort believers.

3. Personal answers.

4. (a) That God Himself was David's place of refuge and part of his inheritance. God understood him and his problems when no one else could. (b) That God hear his prayer and deliver him from those who persecuted him. (c) David's response followed the principle recorded in Philippians 4:6 and 7 because the principle is for believers not to be anxious about anything, but instead, to be thankful and to ask God for every need. (d) That God would "deal bountifully" with him, or hear and answer his prayer.

5. Answers will vary.

6. God cares about the tiniest details of His creation; therefore, He surely cares about the tiniest details of His children's lives.

7. (a) Asa relied upon the Lord for the victory. (b) Show Himself strong on their behalf.

8. *Psalm 34:9*—Those that fear God will not lack for anything. *Psalm 103:11*—God is merciful to those who fear Him. *Psalm 115:11*—God helps

and protects those who fear Him. *Psalm 145:19*—God hears and answers
the prayers of those who fear Him. *Proverbs 9:10*—Those who fear God
grow in wisdom, knowledge, and understanding. *Proverbs 14:26*—Those
who fear God grow confident in His care. *Proverbs 14:27*—Those who fear
God avoid being entrapped by evil and its consequences.

9. God sees and delivers believers from all fears, troubles, and afflictions.

10. God saw how the people were being mistreated, and He heard their cry.

11. Brutish/senseless.

12. God fills the entire heavens and earth; there is nowhere to hide from Him. Nothing obstructs His view of us.

13. God sees everything. All is exposed to His sight.

14. Believers' labor of love on behalf of other believers.

15. He will reward them openly.

16. When we choose to humble ourselves, God lifts us up, or rewards us.

17. He promises that things will go well for them.

Lesson 6

1. God promised to make a covenant with Abram, greatly multiply his descendants, to make many nations of his descendants, and to make kings from among his descendants.

2. God wanted Abraham to remember that God has the power to do what He promises to do.

3. (a) Why did you laugh? Is there anything too hard for God? (b) God exposed her unbelief and hidden thoughts.

4. Isaac repeated the promises that God had made to his father, Abraham.

5. The theme of these verses is God's blessings. It is developed through the repeated words "give you," "blessed me," "shall bless thee," and "blessings."

6. The "Son of man," "the Lord" Jesus Christ.

7. He requires them to be separate from fellowship or close

association with "unbelievers," "infidel[s]," and "idols."

8. *Psalm 46:1*—God is present to give believers help and strength in times of trouble. *Psalm 147:3*—God heals our broken hearts. *Matthew 28:20*—Jesus is always with us. *John 3:16*—Anyone who believes and puts their trust in Christ's sacrifice on Calvary is saved. *John 6:40*—Believers have eternal life. *John 10:28, 29*—No one can take us out of God's hand of protection. *Romans 8:38*—Nothing can separate us from God's love. *1 Corinthians 10:13*—God is faithful to always provide a way of escape in times of trial. *Ephesians 1:3*—God has blessed believers with spiritual blessings. *1 Thessalonians 4:16, 17*—Christ will come again for Christians.

9.

Passage	Believer's Responsibility	God's Promises
Matthew 7:7	To ask, seek from God.	That the believer will find what he or she needs.
Galatians 5:16	To live in harmony with God's Word/to obey God; to walk in the power of the Spirit, not in the power of the flesh.	That the believer will not be controlled by sinful human desires.
Galatians 6:9	To not get tired of doing good, but to keep doing good.	That He will eventually reward the believer.
Philippians 4:6, 7	To not be worried about anything; to pray about everything; to ask God for all he or she needs; to be thankful.	That He will give the believer peace of mind unknown to those who do not believe.
Colossians 3:23, 24	To serve the Lord by serving others.	That He will reward the believer.

Passage	Believer's Responsibility	God's Promises
James 4:10	To submit (humble him- or herself) to God's work in his or her life.	That in time He will exalt the believer.
2 Peter 1:2–4	To be diligent to increase in knowledge concerning God and Christ; to learn the promises of the Bible.	That He will give the believer grace and peace. God will transform the believer's character to reflect His.

10. God is good to those who know Him as their Savior, all of the time, every day. His goodness and blessings to us are beyond our comprehension. God loves His children!

11. He did not believe the message that the angel brought from God.

12. Mary believed the angel, but wanted to know how she would conceive a child without a husband.

13. Sometimes those with the most faith are those who are young and trusting.

14. (a) Mary chose to stay at the house. Martha ran to meet the Lord as He approached their home. (b) She believed that Christ could bring her brother back to life. (c) Jesus told Martha that her brother would rise from the dead. He told her that He had the power over death and that those who believe/trust in Him will never die. (d) Answers will vary.

Lesson 7

1. Baalzebub.

2. *Psalm 148:13*—excellent. *Psalm 145:21*—holy. *Psalm 72:19*—glorious. *Psalm 66:2*—honor.

3. He will not ignore their misuse of His name, but will hold the offenders responsible for their sin.

4. *Psalm 139:20*—God's enemies. *Psalm 74:10*—The adversary/ enemy.

5. *Psalm 89:7*—Saints. *Psalm 111:9*—God's people.

6. Answers will vary.

7. God Almighty.

8. "I am the LORD your God."

9. Merciful, gracious, long-suffering, abundantly good, truthful, just.

10. God's love—all that the name "Jehovah" represents.

11. It is a gift that God paid for, offered freely to all.

12. God delivered Israel from the bondage of slavery by His power. God delivers believers from the penalty and bondage of sin by His power.

13. A guarantee is an assurance for the fulfillment of a condition; for example, "an agreement by which one person undertakes to secure another in the possession or enjoyment of something."

14. "A usually formal, solemn, and binding agreement; a written agreement or promise usually under seal between two or more parties especially for the performance of some action."

15. "Will bring," "did swear," "will give," "am."

16.

Passage	Who	What
Genesis 2:16, 17	Adam	If you disobey, you will surely die.
Genesis 12:1–3	Abram	You will be a great nation. I will bless you. I will make your name great. You will be a blessing. I will bless you. I will curse those who curse you. I will bless all the families of the earth through you.
Genesis 15:2–5	Abram	You will have a son of your own that will be the heir.
Genesis 28:13–15	Jacob	I will give you and your descendants the land. Your descendants will be numerous. The families of the earth will be blessed through your descendant. I will be with you. I will bring you into this land. I will not leave you. I will fulfill my promises to you.
Exodus 6:7	Israelites	I will make you my own people. I will be your God. I will make you know I am your God who delivers you.

Passage	Who	What
Deuteronomy 29:1, 10–15	Children of Israel	God will establish a relationship with you as His people and He your God.
1 Chronicles 17:11–13; 2 Chronicles 6:16	David	I will establish the kingdom of your descendant. I will help him build a house for My name. I will bless his descendants after him. I will be to him as a father. I will not withdraw my mercy from him. The promised Messiah will come from your descendant and His kingdom will be established forever.

17. (a) Thy (your); thee, thou (you). (b) Redeemer. (c) Teaches; leads.

18. (a) Jesus. (b) The Bible calls Jesus all of these things (King of Israel, Lord of hosts, first and last [Alpha and Omega]; God).

19. Jesus Himself established the fact that the Old Testament talks about Him and reveals Him.

Lesson 8

1. (a) He said, "The LORD is with thee," and He called Gideon a "mighty man of valour." (b) Basically he asked, Why is all this happening to us? (c) Answers will vary. It is not wrong to ask why, if we ask in a right spirit and for right reasons, such as to learn what we might be thinking or doing in error; but it is wrong to demand reasons or to ask in unbelief.

2. (a) "Have not I sent thee? . . . Surely I will be with thee." (b) His reason was that his family was poor and that within his family, he was the lowest in importance. (c) "Peace be unto thee; fear not: thou shall not die." (d) Answers will vary.

3. Thoughts of peace.

4. Jesus.

5. Through the blood of the cross.

6. Justification, or forgiveness.

7. No one is righteous, no one seeks for the true God.

8. The middle wall of partition between ourselves and God.

9. "Peace be to this house."

10. "Peace be unto you."

11. "Peace" is the common word in them all: *Romans 1:7*—Grace to you and peace from God our Father, and the Lord Jesus Christ. *2 Peter 1:2*—Grace and peace be multiplied unto you through the knowledge of God, and of Jesus our Lord. *2 John 1:3*—Grace be with you, mercy, and peace, from God the Father, and from the Lord Jesus Christ, the Son of the Father, in truth and love. *Jude 1:2*—Mercy unto you, and peace, and love, be multiplied. *Revelation 1:4*—Grace be unto you, and peace, from him which is, and which was, and which is to come; and from the seven Spirits which are before his throne.

12.

Passage	*Condition to Be Fulfilled*
Psalm 119:165	Love God's Word.
Isaiah 26:3	Keep your mind on God.
Isaiah 32:17	Live righteously.
Isaiah 48:18	Obey God's Word.
Romans 15:13	Believe God's Word.
2 Corinthians 13:11	Live in peace with others.
2 Peter 1:2	Gain knowledge of God, Christ.

13. (a) They feared for their lives because they were in a severe storm. (b) He was not afraid and had absolute confidence in the Father. (c) That He is God and had power over that storm and over every storm in their lives. (d) Jesus has absolute control over the storms in our lives. We can rely on Him.

14. Knowing the love of Christ in a mature way.

15. Peace is produced when the believer walks in the Spirit (i.e., lives in dependence upon the Holy Spirit and in obedience to His Word).

16. (a) Always rejoice in the Lord. (b) Do not be anxious about anything. (c) Pray about everything. (d) Be thankful when you pray. (e) Think about things that are true, honest (honorable), ("just") right, pure, lovely, of good repute, ("virtue") excellent, and worthy of praise. (f) Practice what you have heard and learned.

Lesson 9

1. (a) He feeds his flock; He will make sure they are nourished physically and spiritually. He carries the lambs in His arms; He knows when you or I need to be carried and drawn close to Him. He gently leads pregnant ewes; He will not push you or me faster or farther than we are able to go. (b) Both verses teach that God is faithful and knows our limitations, just as the shepherd knows the limitations of his sheep. God provides a way for us to endure, just as the shepherd helps the sheep who are weak or small.

2. "That great shepherd of the sheep."

3. Christ is willing to sacrifice everything and endure unspeakable suffering to rescue one lost sheep, or soul. We who are the sheep, meanwhile, rebel against God and follow our own sinful desires, even though Christ took upon Himself the punishment for our sins.

4. He described our condition: We were all sinful and lost rebels who wanted to follow our own ways instead of God's. When we trusted Christ as our Savior, we came to the Shepherd who forgave us our sin, made us His own, and took us into His care.

5. Jesus is the shepherd, or caregiver of His own sheep, who are believers. He knows each of His own and calls each by name. Those in His flock recognize His voice, trust Him, and follow Him. Having lived a victorious life that demonstrated how believers are to live, He leads us with His Word and presence. Because we know our own Shepherd, we reject anyone who might lead us astray, and we run from them.

6. Because He gave His life for His sheep.

7. *Verse 13*—Protection. *Verse 14*—Guidance. *Verses 15, 16*—Provision. *Verse 52*—Guidance. *Verse 53*—Protection. *Verse 54*—Provision. *Verse 55*—Protection and provision.

8. (a) "He maketh me to lie down in green pastures." (b) *Psalm 4:8*—Rest, because David said that he lay down to sleep in peace and safety. *Psalm 145:16*—Nourishment, because David said that God satisfies the desire of every living thing. Food and water are two of life's necessities.

9. (a) "He leadeth me beside the still waters." (b) *Isaiah 49:10*—"They shall not hunger nor thirst"; "by the springs of water shall he guide them." *John 6:35*—"I am the bread of life"; "shall never thirst."

10. (a) "He restoreth my soul." (b) *Psalm 86:5*—"Art good, and ready to forgive; plenteous in mercy. *Psalm 56:13*—"Delivered my soul"; "deliver my feet from falling."

11. (a) "He leadeth me in the paths of righteousness for his name's sake." (b) *Psalm 32:8*—"I will instruct thee"; "teach thee"; "I will guide." *Psalm 48:14*—"He will be our guide."

12. (a) "Yea, though I walk through the valley of the shadow of death, I will fear no evil: for thou art with me." (b) *Matthew 28:20*—"I am with you alway." *Hebrews 13:5*—"I will never leave thee, nor forsake thee."

13. (a) "Thy rod and thy staff they comfort me." (b) *Proverbs 3:12*—"He correcteth." *Jeremiah 31:3*—"I have loved thee with an everlasting love"; "with lovingkindness have I drawn thee."

14. (a) "Thou preparest a table before me in the presence of mine enemies." (b) *Psalm 5:11*—"Thou defendest them." *Psalm 18:17*—"He delivered me."

15. (a) "Thou anointest my head with oil; my cup runneth over." (b) *Hebrews 4:16*—"Throne of grace, obtain mercy, find grace to help." *Psalm 147:3*—"He healeth . . . and . . . bindeth their wounds."

16. (a) "Surely goodness and mercy shall follow me all the days of my life." (b) *Psalm 36:7*—"How excellent is thy lovingkindness." *James 5:11*—"The Lord is very pitiful and of tender mercy."

17. (a) "And I will dwell in the house of the LORD for ever." (b) *Hebrews 11:16*—"He hath prepared for them a city." *John 14:2, 3*—"Many

mansions"; "I go to prepare a place for you"; "I will come again"; "Where I am, there ye may be also."

18. He does not care about the sheep.

19. The others were seeking their own interests, not the concerns of Christ.

20. *Psalm 79:13*—By giving thanks. *Ezekiel 34:6*—By searching for lost sheep. *Psalm 95:6, 7*—By worshiping. *Psalm 89:1*—By singing of the Lord's mercies forever; by making His faithfulness known to all generations.

Lesson 10

1. (a) He humbled himself and worshiped. (b) Submissive. (c) He obeyed immediately.

2. First, that there is a God in Israel. Second, that "the LORD saveth not with sword and spear." And, third, that the battle is the Lord's.

3. For our benefit, as examples intended to admonish, warn, and teach us.

4. *1 Peter 2:11*—Fleshly lusts. *1 John 2:15–17*—The world, lust of the flesh, lust of the eyes, and the pride of life. *1 Peter 5:8*—The Devil. *2 Corinthians 4:4*—The Devil, who blinds the unsaved to the gospel. *Galatians 5:17*—The sinful human nature.

5. As more than conquerors.

6. Through God, Jesus Christ.

7. (a) Do not do anything to avenge yourself. (b) If your enemy is hungry, feed him; if he is thirsty, give him a drink; do not be overcome by evil, but overcome evil with good.

8. He will be happy.

9. The Devil flees.

10. In all areas ("things").

11. (a) Faith. (b) Faith.

12. The battle plan is for believers to reject human reasoning and arguments and to make every thought consistent with the knowledge of Christ.

13. The Word of God.

14. The Word of God.

15. James was speaking on behalf of Christian workers who were being cheated by wealthy employers. James implied that the employers ought to be afraid of the judgment of God, the One who has authority to rule and judge.

16. When we treat a Christian wrong, we are treating the Lord wrong. He has the power and authority to judge mistreatment.

17. Answers will vary.

18. He blinds their minds, keeps them in darkness, and entraps them in his lies.

19. By encouraging us to live in sin (vv. 1–6, 9), to not forgive (vv. 7, 10), and to not love (v. 8).

Lesson 11

1. He humbled himself, admitting he was a sinner in need of God's mercy.

2. In God's name and righteousness.

3. Jesus.

4. Jesus.

5. Jesus.

6. No one is righteous, all have sinned.

7. The Lord (Jehovah).

8. We are all as an unclean thing, and all our righteousnesses (morally right actions) are as filthy rags.

9. Being justified by faith, we have peace with God through our Lord Jesus Christ.

10. By the faith of Jesus Christ; by believing/trusting in Jesus Christ.

11. He was wounded to take the penalty for our transgressions.

12. (a) His righteousness. (b) Jesus Christ.

13. The righteous. (Those who are saved have trusted in God's righteousness.)

14. Because they presumed they could stand before God in their own

righteousness and refused to rely upon the righteousness of God alone.

15. Believe in our hearts that God hath raised him from the dead. Call upon the name of the Lord Jesus Christ.

16. The glory of His grace.

17. (a) Paul rejected his own righteousness, which was attained by keeping God's law. (b) He valued the righteousness that he received by faith in Christ alone.

Lesson 12

1. (a) Good master. (b) He did not yet believe that Jesus is the Messiah. (c) Jesus wanted the young man to know that He is God, not simply a good teacher.

2. (a) "My Lord and my God." (b) Thomas was acknowledging his submission to Christ, and his belief that Jesus was not only God, but also his personal God.

3. (a) "Lord, Lord." (b) Answers may vary. The title means "master" and implies that the one using it is willing to submit to the one addressed as "lord." The people called Jesus "Lord," but did not obey Him.

4. (a) Elohim is translated "God." (b) Yahweh/Jehovah is translated as either "Lord" or "God." (c) Adonai is translated "Lord."

5. (a) "Rabboni," or "Master." (b) Answers may vary. Mary expressed her adoration and submission to Christ in using this name.

6. All authority.

7. We are not to call any person Master or Father in the sense that they supersede the authority of Christ.

8. That person trusts God and is blessed (made happy).

9. (a) God is just, righteous, and trustworthy. (b) There is no other God or Savior.

10. God, the blessed and only potentate (ruler); the King of Kings and Lord of Lords.

11. Repent.

12. We are happy.

13. They served/ministered to the saints (other believers).

14. (a) "My Lord" (Adonai). (b) "Thy servant."

15. *Exodus 4:10–13*—Moses, a servant of the Lord. *Psalm 18:1*—David, a servant of the Lord. *Romans 1:1*—Paul, a servant of Jesus Christ. *Romans 16:1*—Phebe, a servant of the church at Cenchrea. *James 1:1*—James, a servant of God and of the Lord Jesus Christ. *2 Peter 1:1*—Simon Peter, a servant and an apostle of Jesus Christ. *Jude 1:1*—Jude, the servant of Jesus Christ.